T0197324

WARRIOR WOMAN

Experiencing Victory Through Everyday Struggles

HEATHER RODIN

WESTBOW
P R E S S®
A DIVISION OF THOMAS NELSON
& ZONDERVAN

WestBow Press books may be ordered through
booksellers or by contacting:

WestBow Press
A Division of Thomas Nelson & Zondervan
1663 Liberty Drive
Bloomington, IN 47403
www.westbowpress.com
844-714-3454

Scripture quotations taken from The Holy Bible, New International
Version® NIV® Copyright © 1973 1978 1984 2011 by Biblica,
Inc. TM. Used by permission. All rights reserved worldwide.

Scripture taken from The Message. Copyright © 1993, 1994, 1995, 1996,
2000, 2001, 2002. Used by permission of NavPress Publishing Group.

ISBN: 978-1-6642-2475-9 (sc)
ISBN: 978-1-6642-2476-6 (e)

Print information available on the last page.

WestBow Press rev. date: 03/19/2021

IN APPRECIATION

I know every manuscript published does not happen without the contribution of many talented people, and this one is no different. But there are some in particular that have gone above and beyond to help this project reflect the heart and soul of the message with efficacy.

Judi Peers has been a mentor, a cheerleader, my sounding board and coach throughout this journey, challenging me to write better, work harder, and dream bigger.

Thank you my friend. You are truly a blessing in my life.

I'm also grateful to my kids, Heidi, Mandi, Pete, Becki, Mike and TJ for letting me share their experiences in illustrations and stories to make this book better. Becki, thankfully your continued push to write this just got too difficult to ignore!

And I can't forget my amazing husband Gord. Baby, your patience, prayers and encouragement mean the world to me.

I love you all.

Heather

An Invitation

Hello, dear sisters. I want to tell you something important.

Father God loves His daughters. You are precious to Him.

God wants His girls to walk confidently in His love, accepting our role as women who are privileged, protected, and powerful. He designed us to be fearless and victorious in the battle against forces of evil!

Although this sounds daunting, God has not left us to fight alone. He sees our struggles and longs for us to discover freedom, so He walks with us, engaging the enemy alongside us.

But why a gender specific book on spiritual warfare? Let me explain.

I have six children—three girls, and three boys. In the 25+ years of raising young'uns, I hosted over 100 birthday parties. During the little girls' parties, they would sit and braid each other's hair, nibble at snacks, and chat about school, make-up, clothes, and boys. But at the boys' parties, they packed in copious amounts of food while holding contests to see who could burp the longest, fart the loudest, spit the farthest, wrestle the strongest, or run the fastest.

There is more than merely a physical difference! And even when we're grown, differences remain. Generally speaking, women need to share feelings but men don't. We cry at movies; men seldom do. We read the instructions, but for men, it's the last resort. We stop for directions when we're lost, while most men refuse. And even though men can find the tiniest tool in a bulging toolbox, they can't seem to find something in the fridge, lol! Women react differently, see things differently, *feel* things differently, enjoy different things, and struggle with different issues, so our spiritual journey is bound to reflect that.

Satan knows these defining differences. He studies us carefully. He watches us intently. He listens to us continually. He learns our natural bent, our inclinations, and our weaknesses. Then he prepares personalized ways to draw us into sin.

Although God's victory over the enemy has already been won on the cross, the battle is not done. We will see in Ephesians 6 our call to step up, stand our God-given ground, retrieve what the enemy is stealing from us, and watch him retreat.

My references are from women in the Bible and throughout my own life journey. We'll learn from Scripture, from the wisdom and writing of great men and women of God, and from our own personal experiences with warrior women who have walked in and out of our lives. This promises an unfolding of God's purposes and plans for His beautiful, feminine creation. (I must add, in this age of gender diversity and identification, we also see a tremendous variety of uniqueness. I am not addressing those issues here. It's outside my expertise.)

I am inviting you to make this journey with your heart open to hear from God. I want you to see His provision for your freedom. I'm inviting you to discover victory through the struggles and joy through the troubles, supernaturally enabled to live in peace and power. I am inviting you to become warrior women, armed and dangerous, ready to march into spiritual warfare, and live as more than conquerors.

So are you ready to breathe in this life-changing adventure? Are you excited to hear from your Creator as He challenges and prepares you? Great! Grab your pen and notebook, a fresh cup of coffee, and let's go.

Jeremiah 9:20 *"Now, O women, hear the word of the Lord; open your ears to the words of his mouth."*

Contents

Chapter One
The Enemy Among Us

The path of soft moss and sweet grass felt cool beneath her bare feet, while the sun warmed her exposed shoulders. There was no hurry in her walk—no stress in her lovely face. As her hips swayed with relaxed steps, the gentle swish of her long hair brushed across her back. She was perfection.

All about her was beauty: fig trees laden with ripened fruit, vines bowing with lush clusters of crimson grapes, branches hanging low from ample mangoes, avocado, papaya, and sweet, fragrant peaches. Birds bedecked in feathers of spring green and indigo blue swooped past, and the soulful song of the nightingale enchanted the forest. Flowers, resplendent in majestic colors, adorned the earthen floor, calling to be smelled, enjoyed, and delighted in. She reached to pick a brilliant ruby hibiscus and tucked it behind her ear. All about her existed beauty and peace, perfection and abundance.

She settled to rest against the smooth trunk of a large apple tree. The umbrella branches cast refreshing shade, and she pulled up her long legs and wrapped her bare arms about them. Her eyes followed a romping baby lamb, bouncing about a lazy lion yawning in the sun. The majestic creature took every opportunity to lick the lamb's soft, delicate face. The lamb bleated with joy in response, then curled up within the lion's large paws and quickly fell asleep. The mesmerizing sound of a nearby creek trickling over jasper stones lulled the woman into deep restfulness. She sighed contentedly and closed her eyes.

"Why are you sitting here sleeping?" The unfamiliar voice jolted her awake. She turned her head to see a beautiful snake arching toward her from the lowest branch of the massive tree. His bulging eyes locked onto hers, and she was drawn to the creature.

"I...I'm not sleeping, I'm enjoying the garden and resting," she yawned.

"You must be faint from hunger," the serpent drawled. "Why aren't you eating this magnificent fruit? Look at it." The snake curled up to expose a round, enticing piece ready for picking. "Did God tell you not to eat anything in His garden?"

"God said we may eat from anything in the garden except this one tree," she responded. "The man said we should not even touch it or we will die."

"Hah! That is not the truth! You will not die. God just said that because He knows if you do eat it, you will know all there is to know. You will know what He knows. You will know good and evil. You will be like God and know everything!"

The woman looked longingly at the tempting piece of fruit. The longer she gazed at the forbidden, the more she desired it. Her mind quickly blocked out all the beauty around her and the many varied things she was allowed to eat and enjoy. Now all she wanted was what she could not have. She reached up and touched the fruit, waiting to see what would happen. Nothing. She did not die. *Well*, she thought, *if that didn't come true, perhaps all the other things God said are not true either. Maybe He really doesn't want good things for us. Could it really_make us as wise as God? How wonderful it would be to know everything!*

As her hand plucked the food and lifted it to her mouth, the snake writhed in anticipation. She took a generous bite, causing sweet nectar to run down her hand. It tasted so good, yet...something wasn't right. There was an inner struggle beginning in her soul—an uncomfortable, foreign stirring. She turned to find the man standing beside her.

His familiar tanned body was a solace to her inner distress. "Husband," she said, "I have something for you." He leaned toward her, noticing the half-eaten piece of fruit in her hand. "Try this," she encouraged. "It is sweet to taste, and I did not die!"

Without thought or question, the man reached for the food and took a large bite.

In an instant, truth crushed like a sledgehammer on ice. Now they did know everything, and it was not good. They knew they had been deceived. They knew they had sinned. They suddenly understood good from evil. And they knew God was not going to be happy. Realization dawned. Everything their Father had said would happen was going to happen.

In that moment, they saw they were naked, and they quickly cut fig leaves to fashion a covering for their exposed bodies.

That afternoon when Father God came for their usual walk, they hid. The man and woman felt shame and guilt for the first time in their lives. And those feelings made them afraid—another unfamiliar emotion.

When God appeared before them, He asked the man, "Did you eat what I told you not to eat?" The man blamed the woman. God asked the woman, "What have you done?" She blamed the serpent.

According to Genesis 3:14-19, God had a lot more to say. It was not going to go well for the man and the woman. They were banned from the incredible garden and sent out into the wilderness to survive. A darkness was about to cover the earth and all that would dwell within it. The beginning had ended, and the end had begun.

How many times have we thought about our sister Eve, wishing she had not listened to what we now know was the devil in snake form? Why had she disobeyed God, taken that fruit, and brought sin into the world? Why would she do that? What was she thinking?

I've learned some interesting facts about sister Eve. In Hebrew, the name God gave Eve is *Ezer Kenegdo. Ezer* means helper, life-saver, giver of life, or rescuer. That term for helper is used seventeen times in the Bible to refer to God's help and strength in a time of need. It is also used three times in the Bible referring to the rescuing help from a military ally. *Kenegdo* suggests comparability and equality. I believe the name for the first human woman was given to show God's design for us as soldiers, lifesavers, helpers, and rescuers for those He places in our life. He is saying we are not beneath His male creation, but are to work side by side, supporting each other—perhaps in different roles, but equal in God's eyes. That makes me smile.

I ran a short survey on Facebook asking this question: "Why do you think Satan tempted Eve and not Adam?" The responses were so good! They were thought provoking and sent me to Scripture to research their statements. Let me share some with you.

It was Satan's first attempt to put Eve in a "lesser" place, knowing future generations would hold her responsible, demeaning women throughout the ages. Satan still tries to keep women thinking they are less.

Satan knew the powerful influence women have over men, especially their husbands, and knew if he could get Eve, he would have Adam too. (Yikes... good to remember!)

Eve was not as strong alone as she would have been with her helpmeet at her side, so Satan waited until she was by herself. A solid partnership certainly offers strength.

Eve was deceived, which means given a false impression. She believed a lie about God's instructions. God did not say they would die if they "touched" the fruit, only when they ate the fruit. Satan used that faulty belief when she touched it and did not die to make her think that perhaps everything else God said was not true either. He still does that today!

When Eve gave the fruit to Adam, he took it without any trickery or seduction. He did not consider God's commands as Eve had. Perhaps if Satan had given it

5

to Adam first, Eve would not have followed. That is a nice thought.

Eve was beguiled, meaning tricked. It was her first encounter with deceit, and she didn't recognize it. Satan was able to trick her with flattery, dissatisfaction, and enchanting ways. She did not check with God first, just gave in to her desires. (Interesting! I'm pretty sure Satan still uses that one on us!)

We can't be sure why the serpent chose Eve, but these responses beg a deeper search into our own lives to see if Satan could have any success using the same wiles with us. So let's have a closer look at four of those responses.

We know that God made Eve an equal partner to Adam. She was created from his rib, not his foot. Eve would walk beside her man, not behind him. Women are not less than men in God's eyes. We are certainly different but never less. Peter does refer to us as a weaker vessel (1 Peter 3:7), and before you get your hormones in a tizzy, just think for a moment. We know we aren't weaker in spirit. We aren't weaker in faith. We aren't weaker in resolve over those under our care. And we aren't weaker in knowledge or understanding. But have you ever asked your son or husband or male friend to open that jar of pickles or carry in the heavy groceries or move a piano or tow your car? We can certainly agree, there are times when we lean on men's strength.

Having someone in our lives to help us be accountable in our faith is a good thing. Whether it is a husband, a friend, a parent, or a pastor, we are stronger when we have someone by our side.

What worked so many years ago still works today. Satan attempts to trick us, using tactics on women such as insecurity, loneliness, dissatisfaction, confusion, depression, fear of failure, and not being enough. Sometimes he just plain tells us God must be wrong! Satan whispers lies into our minds like, *"You are such a loser, you can never do anything right, who would love someone like you. God could never forgive what you did."* Lies, all of them!

What happened to Eve was a focus shift. She stopped looking at what God had given them, His goodness and provision, and began to focus on the one thing He had withheld. No longer counting her blessings, she became obsessed with what had *not* been given. To put it clearly, she allowed a selfish whim to ruin her relationship with a loving, giving, gracious God. (Ouch.)

Let's face it, Satan has always had a lot of schemes and ploys up his sleeve. He studies us, and learns our weaknesses. He will use them to cast doubts and convince us that truth is a lie and lies are truth. How on earth can we fight that?

I believe if we know God's Word, study it, memorize it, and share it, Satan will not find us an easy prey when he seeks to confuse us about what God has said, what Jesus taught, what has been written, and who God is.

In World Wars I and II, the western world and its allies engaged in tremendous efforts to fight ferocious enemies threatening our freedom. The preparation for this endeavor was not taken lightly. A plan was put in place.

The enemy was studied infinitesimally. Military leaders scrutinized every detail of videos showing the adversary's preparations and strategies in war. In order to win, it was important to know as much about the enemy as possible—not just to resist, but to fight back and win.

Soldiers—called to action and well trained in military moves—were deployed around the world. Countries prepared to sacrifice for the sake of peace and freedom.

It was intense. Those battles raged for years filled with days of struggle, of personal cost, of questioning decisions, and at times of a fear we were not winning. The enemy was strong and vicious, like a monster of great evil. Much sacrifice was required, but taking a stand and standing our ground eventually resulted in victory.

Spiritual warfare is much like that. We are actually living behind enemy lines. Evil is all about us. Danger is imminent. Like any other battle, we need to understand our adversary, his dark kingdom, and his schemes, maneuvers, and battery fire in order to know how to fight him successfully.

Even sports teams study their competition with research videos, inside knowledge, and other ways of gaining information about their plays and strategies. If you don't plan to win, you probably won't. You need to know as much as possible about your adversary.

God does not want us to be uninformed. Scripture gives us a lot of detail about Satan's methods of attack so we can be ready, equipped, and confident in our battle plan.

Perhaps you doubt if Satan can really attack Christians. Aren't we protected from that once we are redeemed? Isn't this concept just a fear tactic? Why would a loving God allow that to happen?

Scripture is clear. As children of the Most High God, Satan can never completely possess us. We have the Holy Spirit living in us, and nothing will make Him leave. But Satan is always looking for access to a Christian, and there are things we *do*, *say*, or *believe* that will give him permission to oppress us. He uses things we allow in our lives like ugly words we speak, dark thoughts we dwell on, unforgiveness and resentment, a critical spirit, or an attitude of pride. If we don't deal with these, they continually grow stronger until our thoughts become habits and are much harder to identify and dispose of. Then these and many others give him an opening. Once he's there, he'll dig in and work at gaining greater ground.

We've seen Scripture describe Satan as the "father of lies," the "accuser," the "great deceiver," and the "tempter." He can be any or all of these in his attacks on us. He doesn't want us to know who we are in Christ, nor the power and authority given to us, because if we don't use the weapons God provides and exert power over that old serpent, he will do his best to thwart and control us.

The enemy's goal is to push us away from God. If he can make us feel like there is no help for our problems or twist Scripture in our minds to be more like an accusation than an assurance, we'll become angry with God and other Christians, destroying any relationship that helps us walk in spiritual victory.

One of Satan's greatest strategies is to control our minds. Our mind is the greatest battleground of all. If he can control what we think, it isn't long before he controls our words and our actions. This is where you see the enemy working hard, because it's where he does his best work.

His attacks place wrong thoughts and false beliefs into our minds. His whispers push our buttons to make us angry or jealous or depressed or anxious. And because we don't recognize them for what they are, we allow those dark and debilitating thoughts to remain and grow.

Sometimes Satan has been controlling our thoughts for so long we think they are just bad habits or inherited faults or, worse, we're entitled to think them! And when he has a foothold, he strikes hard and often. When he is successful, his strongholds in our life give permission for his evil spirits to set up lodging, working day and night to keep us oppressed and defeated. Our spiritual life is not going to change until our thoughts do. We won't see victory until we take steps to deal with this monster.

It can start as a minute-by-minute battle to get rid of him, but will be worth the freedom it brings when he loses his grip and has to pack his bags and get out!

As learning Satan's strategies and plans allow us to set up our defense tactics laid out in Scripture, so the reverse also applies. His victories in us over the years has allowed him to learn a lot about us and our weaknesses.

He knows negative thoughts change our behaviors. He realizes resentment triggers mean words and knows anger makes us lash out. Satan understands thoughts of low self-esteem bring depression and hopelessness—that pride turns our face from God. Eventually Satan can make us question God's Word. Before long he's coaxed us into addictions, rebellion, unbelief, regret, guilt—and the most destructive—unforgiveness.

The battlefront of our minds is the most difficult to fight yet brings us the greatest freedom when the battle is won.

But Satan is never upfront in his attacks. He is insidious and slippery. For example, if someone from church calls looking for a volunteer to head up a program, the well-meaning lady may say, "We need someone to head up the nursery scheduling and staffing. We prayed about it, and God gave us your name. We know you don't work, so you are perfect for the job! When can you start?"

You instantly bristle, thinking, *Don't they realize I take care of my aging parents, make meals for the local mission, babysit, run my household, do five loads of laundry a day, and struggle with my own health issues? And what a low blow to say God gave them my name!*

Satan whispers, "How dare they? It is so insulting. You should be angry." If we let these thoughts burrow in, they grow and become dark. They can turn into resentment, and you decide if that is all they think of you, you'll take a break from going to church for a while. And *that* is when Satan gains a foothold.

What if we just respond to the misguided lady with a gentle "No, I'm sorry, but I can't commit to that. I have so much to deal with already that I would not be the right person for this job. But thank you for thinking I could do it! That is encouraging to me."

No foothold. And God is honored by your gentle response.

Or perhaps your husband says, "Did you put my favorite shirt in the dryer? I've told you a hundred times not to do that! What were you thinking?"

Your mind immediately reacts. *He has no respect for me and all I have to do. As if I have time to search out this ridiculous shirt when I have so much to wash!* Then you respond with, "If you don't like the way I do your laundry, you can just do it yourself! I'm not your slave!"

Words hurt, and hurting people hurt people. Take a deep breath before reacting caustically and deflect it simply, "Sorry. My mistake." This could save the day. Small things are often big leaps in guarding our hearts and minds and disabling the enemy.

Hurt feelings create footholds, which become strongholds that can develop into broken relationships. It is a slippery slope, and Satan knows just when the hormones are raging and we are overly sensitive. He knows that when we are exhausted, we are vulnerable. He knows if we have been pushed beyond our endurance, we will respond in anger. He knows when we are feeling invincible, we are ripe for a fall. He knows...he knows...and we need to know that he knows and be ready to deal with his attacks.

Chip Ingram's book *The Invisible War* lists five basic truths about spiritual warfare. They are important. As warrior women we need to learn and understand them before engaging the enemy:

• There is an invisible world.
• We are involved in an invisible war.

- Our foe is formidable.
- We must respect our foe but not fear him.
- We do not fight *for* victory. We fight *from* victory.[1]

1 John 4:4 encourages us with, *"You are from God, little children, and have overcome them; because greater is He who is in you than he who is in the world."*

Remember that Satan is a defeated enemy. Jesus has already conquered him through His death on the cross. We are equipped to face the enemy, resist him, and defeat him. We have the armor and weapons God has provided to stand our ground. We are already victorious, valiant, and triumphant!

You may be thinking I can't do this! I'm not strong enough. It's too scary. I've no heart for entering any kind of war. I'll just mess it up somehow, and make things worse.

You're not alone! That has been a common response since the beginning of time. Sarah laughed when the angel told them they would have a son (Genesis 18:15). Moses balked at leading the children of Israel out of Egypt (Exodus 4:10-17). Jonah ran the opposite direction when God called him to go to Nineveh (Jonah 1:3). King Saul actually called a witch for help instead of waiting for a prophet of God (1 Samuel 28). Gideon didn't feel equipped to go to war when God called and asked twice for confirmation before obeying (Judges 6:33-40). But they all ended up seeing the hand of God either in victory when they obeyed, or disaster and destruction when they did not.

---

[1] Chip Ingram, *The Invisible War.* Baker Books, 2015.

I can empathize with these biblical characters. When I felt God call me to write this book on spiritual warfare, I truly felt unworthy and ill equipped—a bit terrified actually. I too felt like running, jumping ship, and asking God to chose another. So, like Gideon, I asked for confirmation, and like Gideon, He gave it, in several ways. God calls His children to do things that look impossible—beyond our natural abilities—so that we must depend on His. Confronting an enemy can be intimidating, but we're learning that with God all things are possible. Right?

"But, what if we fail," you say. "Or worse, end up just waking a sleeping monster?" My friend let me tell you, the monster is not sleeping. He is hard at work in you, your family, and your friends. The time has come to grab our armor, take a stand, stand our ground and stand firm!

We're not done with looking at Satan's tactics, so keep going. Chapter four will take us deeper. But first, we need to see who is in charge!

Questions

Have you ever struggled with a "focus shift" like Eve did, where instead of looking at God's provisions you find yourself consumed with something you don't have? How did that affect your actions? How did that affect your relationships?

Which one of the survey responses speaks to you? Explain. After thinking about it, do you have your own response? Write it out.

Who do you have in your life to be a spiritual support and accountability partner? Take time to thank them and pray for them. If you do not have anyone, use this moment to ask God to provide someone, then wait and see what He will do.

How do you feel about learning that Satan can find access into your life through your thoughts, words, and actions? Is there one of those more apt to be your weakness than another? How does this help you understand issues you battle?

Reread the examples of what our thoughts can lead to, and think of a similar situation in your life you can share. Be honest. Healing comes from confession! What would have been a better response from you?

What pushes your buttons? Think of things that set you off in the areas of anger, self-pity, depression, anxiety, or resentment. Identifying these can help you prepare a better response in advance. Write out a short prayer asking God to help you identify red flags, and ask Him for wisdom to work through these issues.

Chapter Two
The God Who's For Us

The unrelenting heat of the day had drained his energy and the prophet rolled his cloak fashioning a pillow for his bed. Resting his head upon it, slumber quickly claimed him.

"Jonah." The sleeping man stirred. "Jonah! Arise!" The prophet recognized the voice of his God and sat up quickly.

"Yes Adonai? I'm here."

God continued to speak. "Jonah, I've seen the rampant evil of the city of Nineveh. I'm ready to destroy them if they don't repent and turn from their wicked ways, and I'm sending you to go and deliver this message."

The prophet sat in silence for a few moments, then wordlessly put on his wrinkled cloak, picked up his staff and moneybag, and headed out the door. Nineveh lay 500 miles northeast of Israel, but without hesitation, he turned southwest toward Joppa. *Ninevites are the Jews cruelest enemies. They don't deserve God's forgiveness.* His thoughts turned dark. *I am never going to give them God's message. If they repent, Adonai will forgive them, and that must not happen!* The slap of his sandals left puffs of dust as he hurried through the city gates.

Rancid smells of rotten seaweed and dead fish wafted past him, and he knew the seaport was near. There were always trading vessels willing to accept a paying customer, and he planned to be one.

The first ship he saw had a deck loaded with cargo. "My friend," he called to a seaman, "where is your ship headed?"

"We sail for Tarshish in two hours." The scruffy sailor continued to roll a thick rope around his bent, burly arm. "If you want to come, climb aboard and pay your fare!"

Tarshish! That's perfect! As far east as I can go! Jonah climbed the rope ladder, tossed his coins to the captain, and found a quiet corner below deck. Laying his head on a rough, wooden bench, the exhausted prophet fell into a sound sleep.

"Hey you!" The gruff voice carried a tremor. "Get up! How can you sleep through this dreadful storm?"

Jonah started to rub his weary eyes, but instead clutched the edge of the bench as the ship pitched violently. *A storm—every seaman's nightmare!*

The captain stood before him, fear etched across his weathered face. "We are going to perish! So call on whoever your god is, and ask him to save us! We've thrown the cargo into the sea and called on all our gods, but it hasn't helped. Now we need to cast lots to see who is responsible for this storm! Follow me."

The howling wind made it difficult for Jonah to hear the man, but he drew his cloak about him and staggered behind the captain into a small, dank room where the waiting crew huddled.

A clay pot filled with small stones was passed around the circle; each sailor retrieving one. When Jonah drew the black stone, all eyes locked on him, then questions flew. "Who are you?" "Where are you from?" "Who are your people?" "Who is your God, and what have you done to anger Him?"

The raging storm threatened to swallow his words. "I am a Hebrew and I serve the God of heaven who made the sea, and the dry land. I am running away from Him."

The men gasped, their fear tangible as they recoiled in terror. Only the most powerful God could control the sea, and seamen knew *that* God reigned over all things—including their gods.

"What should we do to you to pacify your God, so we may live?"

Jonah's heart sank. "There's only one way. Throw me overboard, and the storm will cease."

The captain and crew tried to row to shore, not wanting to risk angering this God. But the storm screamed with greater force until death was immanent. As shipmates held Jonah over the roiling sea, the captain cried into the wild wind, "Oh powerful God, don't blame us for this man's death. Don't let us drown! Yet, we see You are Almighty God, and will do as You choose!"

The second Jonah's body hit the water, the wind stopped and the sea stilled. The crew immediately fell to their knees. Pressing their faces to the crusty brine on the soaked deck the terror struck seamen worshipped the all-powerful God who restored life and delivered from harm. They offered a sacrifice from what was left in their storeroom, and vowed to serve Him always.

Jonah's limp body slipped silently through the cold, dark water, down, down, down to the bottom of the frigid sea. Weeds wrapped around his face and head, and pain gripped his burning lungs. As darkness closed in, he knew his days were over. *Help me God!* Suddenly the waters swirled about a massive monster swimming toward him. His opened jaws scooped the dying prophet, seaweed and all, inside his vast form.

Jonah tumbled and rolled inside the fish, finally resting inside its rank, cavernous belly. Rancid water and slime sloshed around him as realization dawned. *I'm still alive! Adonai! You heard my prayer!* Sucking in oxygen, the soggy prophet lifted his heart in thanksgiving. *You are truly a gracious and loving God.*

For three days and three nights Jonah lay inside the fish, thinking, wondering, and hoping. His legs were cramped and his eyes could see nothing. The smell was overwhelming and things bumped into him he did not want to identify.

As endless hours passed, images of his disobedience and rebellion against God replayed through his mind. What had made him think he could out smart Elohim?

Adonai, I will worship You always, with thanksgiving and praise, for You are mighty, and greatly to be feared! Adonai, if You save me, I'll obey You and go to Nineveh.

A sudden movement tossed Jonah about. In a flash, Jonah found himself flying through the monster's gaping jaws to land in a heap on a sea-washed shore, along with reeking remnants from the fish's belly.

Struggling to his knees, the disheveled prophet heard God's voice again. "Now go to Nineveh, Jonah, and give them My message to repent."

Jonah cleaned off in the ocean, and went.

On the first day in the great city, Jonah wasted no time. It was going to take at least three days to get from the south gate to the north gate, so he began preaching immediately. "BECAUSE OF YOUR GREAT SINS, NINEVEH WILL BE DESTROYED IN FORTY DAYS UNLESS YOU REPENT! REPENT! REPENT NOW!"

Surprisingly, no one came at him swinging swords or pitching rocks. No one shouted at him to leave their city. Instead, people stopped, and listened. They seemed shaken by his words, and went off whispering among themselves.

The king soon heard of the prophet's message, and trembled. Taking off his royal robes, he wrapped himself in burlap, and sat down in the dirt. "Issue a new declaration!" he bellowed. "No man, woman, child, or animal is to eat or drink anything. We will call on God for forgiveness of our wicked ways, and turn from the despicable things we have all been doing. Perhaps God will hear us, and change His mind." The king grasped at hope. "Maybe His anger will turn from us, and He will let us live!"

As Jonah feared, God saw their repentance. He heard their cries. He regarded the sincerity of their fast, and had compassion on the city. Holy God decided to forgive and not destroy them as He had said He would.

"Adonai! This is exactly why I ran away from You!" Jonah was angry. "I knew You would do this! I know You are gracious and compassionate, not easily angered, full of love and quick to change Your plans of punishment to forgiveness! I did not want this evil city to receive your mercy! I wanted them to suffer as they made the people of Israel suffer! If You won't kill them, You may as well kill me, because I'm better off dead than watching this!"

"Jonah, my son. I have only shown Nineveh what I have shown you: grace, mercy, forgiveness and salvation. You have no right to be angry."

The furious prophet didn't want to hear God's words and stormed out of the city. He went to a nearby hill to watch and pout, sitting under a poor shelter, hastily crafted of leaves to protect from the burning sun.

God regarded his disgruntled servant, knowing his jealous thoughts and resentment, and commanded a shade tree to instantly spring up beside him. The leaves were broad and offered much needed shelter and coolness. Jonah appreciated the reprieve but continued his tantrum.

The next dawn, God sent a worm to kill the tree. As dawn turned to day, a blistering sun beat down on Jonah. Now, the prophet was also riled over the loss of refreshing shade. But God was not finished. "Jonah, what right do you have to get angry about this shade tree? You did not plant it, or water it. You did nothing to bring it into being. I am the giver of all good gifts, and You only had to enjoy it.

In the same way, I give the gift of grace, mercy, compassion and forgiveness to those I chose. I can change My mind at any time as I see fit. I am God, and will continue through all time to do all things in My omniscient, holy, transcending wisdom and power.

Learn of Me, Jonah. Obey Me, and you will see more wonderful things that I can do."

Jonah 1,2,3,4.

I've recounted this story because more than anything else, I long to introduce you to God—Jonah's powerful God! I'm hoping you, like me, will fall before Him in awe, whispering what heavenly beings shout—*"Holy, holy, holy, is the Lord God Almighty. Who was, who is, and who is to come!"* Revelation 4:8

God is so beyond our comprehension that our minuscule understanding of His absolute greatness often hinders our faith and trust. In our attempts to get our mind around who He is, we tend to put Him in a box of our own imagination, which is never, ever close to reality. That little box lulls us into the pseudo-contentment of believing He is actually what we think He is. But our human minds are finite; without revelation from the Holy Spirit, we can't completely see God in all truth. We create a God that is too small. And when He doesn't do what we feel He should, our faith wavers like a sapling in the wind.

A.W. Tozer made a great statement in his book *The Knowledge of the Holy*. He said, "What comes to our mind when we think of God is the most important thing about us." He suggests that a low view of God is the cause of a hundred lesser evils. Without a sense of awe, an appreciation of His majesty, an awareness of His presence, and a desire to worship and pray, the true concept of God is lost and His message to us is less life changing than it should be.[2]

I'm not sure by whom, but I've heard it said, "The greater our God, the smaller our devil." I like that. We need a truer vision—as great an understanding of the Creator as possible. To see God in all His power and majesty as shown

---

[2] A.W. Tozer, *The Knowledge of the Holy.* HarperOne, 1978.

in Scripture is a good way to begin our search for a clearer sense of His glory and power.

It's also hard to know who *we* are until we know more about who God is. For it's in the "not knowing" that our faith is shaken, rendering us vulnerable to the lies of the enemy. Gaining knowledge of God strengthens us and holds us up through the dark days and difficult situations that are sure to come.

God's signature is all around us. We see Him in nature, through the circle of life and death, by revelation of the Holy Spirit, and through divine intervention, but we will learn most profoundly about God through His Word. Scripture. It's there that we see His character, His heart, His plan, and His will. And as we soak in His rich truth, God reveals more. So let's get started!

God is not a created being. The book of Revelation says that God is the Alpha and the Omega, the beginning and the end. He was not made from anything. He has always been and always will be. God told Moses His name was I AM—meaning "eternally existing." (Exodus 3:14)

Psalm 90:2 ESV *"Before the mountains were born or you brought forth the earth and the world, from everlasting to everlasting You are God."*

God is the Creator of all life, visible and invisible, angelic beings, and creatures of the earth, the sea, and the sky. Genesis chapter one gives us a detailed schedule of each step of creation, but it's clear our world began because God wanted us here. He created man and woman in His likeness. Both were an important part of displaying His majestic, perfect, loving entity.

Colossians 1:16 ESV *"For by Him all things were created: things in heaven and on earth, visible and invisible, whether thrones or powers of rulers or authorities; all things have been created through Him and for Him."*

God is three: God the Father, God the Son, and God the Holy Spirit—yet Scripture tells us they are one God. A trinity. *Tri* means three, and *unity* means one. Three different beings in one, like the egg with a shell, the white, and the yolk. Like water being liquid, ice, or steam. Like the sun being light, heat, and radiation. None of these illustrations describe God perfectly, but they do give our limited minds a little understanding. One God as three separate beings— each with unique identity, purpose, and power.

Matthew 28:19 ESV *"Therefore go and make disciples of all nations, baptizing them in the name of the Father and of the Son and of the Holy Spirit."*

God is holy (without sin). God is holy by nature. He hates sin. He hates that it robs us of the life He wants for us in a similar way a mother hates the cancer that steals life from her child.

Since the fall of humanity in the Garden of Eden, we have always been drawn toward evil, toward what we should not be, what we should not do, and what we should not say or think. It's in our glimpse of Holy God that we realize the wickedness in us. In that brief look, we see the opposite of what we see in ourselves and in others. Right then, a longing for change either grips us or repels us. And it is in the heart that longs to be changed that the Holy Spirit works, shaping us into the image we were created to be.

God's holiness extends hope—hope of forgiveness, hope of freedom, and hope of a future and eternal life. God's holiness allows change from our natural bent for evil, to one of being holy as He is holy.

Isaiah 6:3 *"Holy, holy, holy, is the Lord of hosts. The whole earth is full of His glory!"*

God is omniscient, all knowing. We are always learning, but God never learns anything new. He is never surprised. He knows all things accurately in advance and never makes a mistake. He sees the beginning from the end, He is always in control, and He is certainly not sitting in heaven wringing His hands, wondering what can possibly be done to save this planet. He has a perfect plan and will see it through to the very end. That plan is wonderfully laid out for us all the way from Genesis to Revelation! He wants us to know Him and know His plan for us. God won't just win in the end—He is winning now...winning every single day!

1 John 3:20 *"For God is greater than our hearts, and He knows everything."*

Hebrews 4:13 *"Nothing in all creation is hidden from God's sight. Everything is uncovered and laid bare before the eyes of Him to whom we must give account."*

God is omnipotent. This means having power without limit. God must have power to reign, but to reign sovereignly, He must have all power. His power is absolute, and He is the source of all power. God does not exert energy when He works. Nothing tires Him. God doesn't need to rest, recharge, recuperate, or replenish His power. It is unbounded, measureless, and without end.

Matthew 19:26 *"And looking at them Jesus said to them, 'With people this is impossible, but with God all things are possible.'"*

God is omnipresent. He is everywhere all the time and promises to always be with us—no matter what, no matter when, no matter where.

Scripture tells us there is no place in heaven, on earth, or in hell where we can hide from Him. Because God is infinite, His presence is infinite also. God created this world and remains in it to hold it together and keep it going. At the same time, His presence helps us distinguish between good and evil. His presence also offers Christians the ability to have joy even in times of sorrow and be filled with peace and assurance when everything falls apart. His presence allows us to be gentle, patient, and kind when all about us is not.

Psalm 139:7-10 *"Where can I go from Your Spirit? Where can I flee from Your presence? If I go up to the heavens, You are there; if I make my bed in the depths, You are there. If I rise on the wings of the dawn, if I settle on the far side of the sea, even there Your hand will guide me, Your right hand will hold me fast."*

God delights to show us mercy and forgiveness. Mercy is described as benevolence, forbearing, an act of pardon, divine evidence of favor, blessing, clemency, and leniency.

The Hebrew word for *mercy* is a reference to the womb, suggesting the nurturing and protective aspect of God. I love that thought.

God's mercy never ends and never fails. Neither could His mercy ever be greater or less. It is constant. It is a gift from heaven available to all, even though unmerited, and is to be embraced with thanksgiving and joy. It is boundless and free, available at just the moment we need it—but only accessed when accepted by faith.

God's *justice* is dispensed only when His *mercy* is rejected. God is a loving parent who longs to forgive us for all things. Our only part in this is to receive His mercy and forgiveness with a grateful heart.

Micah 7:18 *"Who is a God like You, who pardons sin and forgives the transgression of the remnant of His inheritance? You do not stay angry forever but delight to show mercy."*

God is love. 1 John 4:8 says, *"Whoever does not love does not know God, because God is love."* God isn't just loving, He and love are virtually one and the same thing. His love had no beginning, and it has no end. It is hard for us to understand exactly what pure love is, but we know how it manifests. 1 Corinthians tells us that love does no harm, it casts out evil, it gives freely, it forgives all, it lays down its life for another, and it is bottomless and vast. This is almost impossible to comprehend, but what we do understand is how much we need this love!

God is compassionate, gracious, and slow to anger. When we speak of the compassion and goodness of God, it's His kindness, sympathy, tender heartedness, bestowing of good gifts and blessings, or gentleness. It is His willingness to put our confessed sins as far away as the east is from the west—no longer to exist. Jesus taught and showed this compassion as He lived His life here on earth, giving us a peek at the compassion of the Father and showing the way *we* must strive to live.

Exodus 34:6,7 *"The Lord, the Lord, the compassionate and gracious God, slow to anger, abounding in love and faithfulness."*

God is the giver of all good gifts. Good things come from God, because He is a good, good Father. He longs to bless us. If we take time to count some of those blessings already in our lives, we will be amazed at what we have because of the generosity of God.

James 1:17 *"Every good and perfect gift is from above, coming down from the Father of the heavenly lights."*

God also gives these gifts in perfect ways. His gifts come from various places, events, and people in our lives. God's gifts are given for our good, and in His perfect timing. We may not always recognize situations in our life as good gifts, but in time as we walk in faith, God will reveal events that once seemed insignificant or difficult, as blessings. Joseph's story is a good example. (Genesis 45:4-8.) Because of his brothers' jealousy and violence, Joseph spent up to twelve years in an Egyptian prison waiting for God's plan to unfold. When he saw his brothers many years later, God's plan was revealed.

Genesis 50:20 *"You intended to harm me, but God intended it for good to accomplish what is now being done, the saving of many lives."*

God is patient. As a mother of six children, my patience was tried every day, and sadly, many days it failed. I'm so glad my heavenly Father doesn't fail. I know beyond a shadow of a doubt I try His patience often. I still slip into thoughts or words not honoring to Him, but I also know with a simple confession I'm forgiven, and that spurs me on to do better. And my patience shown toward others pleases Him.

Galatians 5:22 *"But the fruit of the Spirit is love, joy, peace, **patience**, kindness, goodness, faithfulness, gentleness and self-control." (emphasis mine)*

God is just. This attribute works in unity with all His other attributes. I quote A.W. Tozer, who said, "God's compassion flows from His goodness, and goodness without justice is not goodness."[3] God is supreme, and His decisions to punish or forgive are only His to know and understand. Through Jesus' sacrifice of death, God's justice was satisfied and mercy is offered to all who will accept it. When we accept this gift we are pronounced by God as just.

Revelation 15:3,4 *"Great and marvelous are Your deeds, Lord God almighty. Just and true are Your ways, King of the nations. All nations will come and worship before You for Your righteous acts have been revealed."*

But Tozer has more to say. "The vague and tenuous hope that God is too kind to punish the ungodly has become a deadly opiate for the consciences of millions. It hushes their fears and allows them to practice all pleasant forms of iniquity while death draws every day nearer, and the command to repent goes disregarded. As responsible moral beings, we dare not trifle with our eternal future."[4]

---

[3] Tozer, *The Knowledge of the Holy.*
[4] Tozer, *The Knowledge of the Holy.*

There is an essential action required on our part—receiving Jesus, and giving Him control over our lives. Many would rather wallow in their sins than take this step, but Scripture is clear that without it they will be turned away at heaven's gates and sent to hell for eternity.

God does not lie. I lie. I'm a work in progress, but I'm guessing you're shocked to hear that admission. It's horrible, but it's the truth. And here is another one. You lie too. You can shake your head all you want, but you know sometimes a lie or exaggeration just slips out without a thought. Lies always hurt someone. Even though we tell ourselves that the lie did no harm, it has. It hurts God, because He is truth, and lying is offensive to Him. There is no deceit in God. What He says has happened *has* happened. What He says will happen, *will* happen. What He promises, He does, without fail, every time. And God has commanded, we must shed deceit and wear truth.

Romans 3:4 MSG *"Depend on it: God keeps His word even when the whole world is lying through its teeth."*

Hebrews 6:18 *"It is impossible for God to lie."*

God's ways are perfect. God never makes a mistake! He is perfect in the ways He changes us, the ways He leads us, the ways He provides for us, and the ways He heals us. His gifts are perfect, and His disciplines and corrections are always timely and exactly what we need.

2 Samuel 22:31 ESV *"As for God, His way is perfect; the word of the Lord is flawless."*

God loves us and offers us a gift of salvation. We talked briefly about this earlier, but let's look at it again.

While we were still in our sin, before we had even inclined our hearts toward Him, God loved us enough to give His precious Son to save us. This gift of forgiveness offers us heaven instead of hell. It offers us eternal life instead of eternal death.

God has made a way for each of us, but it only becomes reality if we accept it. Like a gift on Christmas morning sitting under the tree, it's ours only when we pick it up and open it. Until then, like God's gift of salvation, it waits with our name on it, but the giving isn't completed until we receive it. God's gift of salvation must be personally accepted.

Yet you may have heard someone say, "Well if all my friends are going to be in hell, then I want to be there too." Wrong. You do not want that, my friend. Hell will be horrible. Hell will be darkness and suffering without the mercies of God. As long as you have breath, you have the chance to accept Jesus' payment for your sin and the promise of eternal life, but the moment your heart stops beating, the opportunity is gone forever. Don't let guilt of past years or behaviors keep you from making this decision. God promises in Joel 2:25 ESV, *"I will repay you for the years the locust have eaten."* Our amazing God will restore our lost days, lost months, or lost years. We can't get those days back, but God will heal, forgive, and make everything going forward new, exciting, and more beautiful than we could ever imagine!

My precious sister, take this moment to make sure you have given your all to Jesus and accepted His death on your behalf. Don't wait. Don't procrastinate. Not one of us knows what tomorrow holds, so please, do it right now.

For anyone wanting to take this step, I'm including a prayer here for you to pray. If God is speaking to you, this is the perfect time. It will be the most important thing you ever do.

Dear Heavenly Father, I humbly bow before You with a heart of thanksgiving for Your gift of eternal life through the death of Your Son, Jesus. I accept what Jesus has done for me and confess all the things in my life that are wrong, selfish, or hurtful. Please forgive my sin, and help me to forgive those who have hurt me. I want eternal life forever with You. Jesus, I give You control of my life and ask You to fill me with Your Holy Spirit that I may walk in obedience. Search me, cleanse me, forgive me, and make me a new creature to live for You, my God and Savior. Amen.

Romans 6:23 *"For the wages of sin is death, but the gift of God is eternal life in Christ Jesus our Lord."*

John 3:16 *"For God so loved the world that He gave His only begotten Son, that if any man, women or child believes in Him, they shall not perish, but have life eternal."*

God will bear our burdens. God wants us to bring our cares and concerns to Him. He wants to carry the heavy load that threatens to bend and break us. He has promised if we do that, He will give us peace in return and fill that space our burdens occupied with abundant life.

Psalm 55:22 ESV *"Cast your cares on the Lord and He will sustain you; He will never let the righteous fall."*

1 Peter 5:7 *"Cast all your anxiety on Him for He cares for you."*

God sings over us. I can't imagine how beautiful God's voice in song would be. The thought gives me shivers.

To envision Almighty God singing over me, over you, is a stirring picture, and speaks to His nurturing love for us.

God planned our entrance into this world long before time began. He knew how many hairs would be on our precious heads and what color they would be (naturally and chemically), and He delights in us.

Zephaniah 3:17 *"The Lord your God is with you, the Mighty Warrior who saves. He will take great delight in you; in His love He will no longer rebuke you, but will rejoice over you with singing."*

Psalm 139:13,15-16 *"For You created my inmost being; You knit me together in my mother's womb...My frame was not hidden from You when I was made in the secret place...All the days ordained for me were written in Your book before one of them came to be."*

Who is like our God? No one. There is none other! He sits on a great throne and rules with truth and justice. God does not need our help; we aren't necessary to Him, yet He who needs no one, *wants us*! In His love, He works in and through us to do good things. To reject this means *we* sit on the throne of our life, stealing it from the Creator who has a right to it and wants to be there. Reigning over our own life, as we will see, cannot bring wholeness, healing, or blessing. It brings disaster.

Exodus 15:11 *"Who among the gods is like You, O Lord? Who is like You—majestic in holiness, awesome in glory, working wonders?"*

In this chapter, we have covered some of God's attributes— but just knowing *about* God is not enough. Even the demons believe in God, and tremble. Our heavenly Father is calling us into a personal relationship with Him, longing to cover us with His love and protection.

I realize the "father image" is not necessarily a pleasant one for everyone. Some have not had a loving, gentle dad in their past, and every time they hear the word *father*, there's an instant bad taste in their mouth, conjuring an uncomfortable response. But regardless of any negative personal experiences with our earthly fathers, our heavenly Father is more than we could hope for or imagine. He knows us, sees us, loves us, and cares for us. He is forgiving and merciful. He is wise and understanding. He is powerful. He is kind. He is gentle. He is what is always longed for in an earthly father, and more.

God is and always will be perfect in all His ways—magnificent, powerful, loving, and completely worthy of our praise.

And God has more for us. We are going to see how He loves us, sees beauty in us, and gave us an identity that will blow your socks off. Are you as eager to learn about that as I was? Well, hang in there. That's coming up in the next chapter. Stay tuned for our story.

Questions

What comes to your mind when you think about God? Don't be afraid to take some time to think this one through. It's important.

Have you ever thought of the fact God planned for you to be born before time even began? That He knew what you would be like and He still wanted you here? How does that encourage you?

How do you relate to God as a loving father?

Looking through the Scriptures that tell us about the character of God, which one are you immediately drawn to? Why?

In Psalm 68:19, we learn God wants to carry our burdens. Is there a burden you are carrying that weighs heavily on you? Can you put it in His hands and let it go? What do you think would happen if you stopped right now and gave that problem to God? This is a good time to do it, my friend! Go ahead! He is waiting. And if you prayed that prayer, please tell someone. Find a fellow believer and share your news! Heaven is rejoicing, and so should you!

In Appendix A at the back of the book you will find more about God, including His many names. Don't forget to take a look.

Chapter Three
Through God's Eyes

The young girl's dress stretched tightly against her too-thin body. Her ankles, snuggly strapped into dusty stilettos, wobbled over the uneven road as she struggled to get to her next customer. She was tired, hungry, and wishing this day would come to an end.

Her name had been changed again. She couldn't remember her real one. She was called Tia now, a name given to her by her latest pimp, along with a few important lessons he felt she should learn.

My eye is still swollen, and that cheap makeup didn't cover up the bruises. With that thought, she hurried to the next place to avoid facing his anger again. The soft breeze cooling her dark skin also carried a beautiful sound.

Is that music? Tia slowed her steps as she neared a small mission. A crowd sat singing on a knoll of sparse grass burnt dry by the scorching sun. It was a song she had never heard.

She watched an elderly Haitian man stand up to speak to the group. His face was kind, his clothes were worn but clean, and his stooped form bespoke gentleness. Forgetting her hurry, she stepped closer to hear him more clearly.

"My fellow villagers, the living God has sent me here to tell you something very important. He wants you to know that He sees you, He hears you, He cares about you, and He loves you. He planned your life before the beginning of time, and He knows your name. The God who created heaven and earth has a great gift to give you if you will receive it. He wants to give you a new life. A life filled with hope instead of sadness, a heart filled with joy instead of sorrow, and a mind filled with peace instead of burdens."

There's a God who sees me and knows my name? Tia wondered. *But why would He love me? I'm...I'm nobody. And give me a life of hope? I have never known that!*

She could barely imagine a different life. She had been in this business since her mother had sold her to an uncle at the age of five. Now there seemed no other way to survive.

Curiosity mixed with desperation propelled her to sit with the others on the knoll.

"This loving God saw our helplessness." The man spoke with authority. "He saw our sins and the darkness in our hearts, and He gave His only Son to die for us so we could have forgiveness and a clean heart. He wants to give us purpose, life that promises heaven after we die, and peace and joy while we remain on this earth. He wants to write your name in His book of life."

Oh! I need all those things! I want God to write my name in His book. Her chest tightened. *But I don't even remember my real name, so how will God know what to write?*

The old man continued, "If you want this new life, you need to come to Jesus, the Son of the living God, who gave His life for you. He will help remove your old life like a dirty garment and fit you with a pure, clean, new one. He will give you power against voodoo curses, and that old serpent Djab will have to leave you be! Come forward, and I will pray with you."

Tia knew well of Djab...Satan. She had been dedicated to him at birth. His mark remained under the skin on her right arm, and the gold ring in her ear told everyone whom she belonged to. But that master had only brought pain. This new master Jesus brought healing, the man said. Could he be right? Could she belong to this wonderful God? Would He want her?

In spite of her questions, Tia's legs furtively moved her toward the old man, falling at his feet. "I want this new life, pastor. I must know this living God and His Son Jesus. I need a different life...one with hope."

The old man slowly sank to the ground beside Tia, showing her verses from his worn Bible that explained God's plan for her life. With a voice as gentle as the coo of a dove, he led the girl to accept Jesus into her heart.

"Now," he said, "you must leave this life you have been living, my daughter. You are God's child now and a new person. If you come live with my wife and me, we will teach you more. You are no longer a servant to Satan and his evil ways. The blood of Jesus redeems you. You are now a child in God's family."

They helped each other up, and he put his thin arm about her trembling shoulders. Turning from the mission, the two made their way down the dirt path. As they walked toward his humble home, he softly asked her name.

She was quiet for a long moment, seemingly deep in thought, then a smile lit her face with remembrance and she whispered, "Lovely. My name is...Lovely."

The identity of a woman of God

The story above is based on a real experience. Lovely's story is a beautiful example of God's love for all women and His heart of grace and mercy toward us. As Christians, we need to pray for those He puts on our hearts. We don't know who God is calling to Himself, and we don't want to miss out on a miracle like Lovely's.

But you've probably noticed the word *Christian* does not carry the good will it once evoked. Instead, the world often spits out the word like a bad mushroom, describing it as something akin to the black plague. God's people have not always represented Him well.

At times in my life, Holy Spirit whispers have asked me, "Are your words and actions righteous or just religious?" It stops me cold in my tracks, and I find myself making corrective steps. I'm not alone. It seems many well-meaning Christians often come across as harsh, judgmental, or uncaring—the reflection of God's grace and mercy missing. And we wonder why the label *hypocrite* gets attached to us!

Why are we so horrible at living out our faith? Perhaps it's because we don't really know who we are as daughters of the King. If we are lost and confused in our identity, we will be lost and confused in our role.

We need to start seeing ourselves as God sees us, and not the way we see ourselves. God does not give us power to be all *we* want to be, He gives us power to be all *He* wants us to be!

The Bible says in 1 Peter 3:15 to be ready with a word to share about that hope within us, for when we live it, people around us see the transformation and will want to know why. Living a God-filled life brings people to Jesus and allows the name *Christian* to be sweet like honey.

Knowing who God says we are can change everything, and when we believe it, it gives us power to be victorious. And dangerous!

Here are some of our identities from God's Word. As you read through them, underline the ones that mean the most to you.

Who are we?

- We are children of the living God, adopted and given His name (John 1:12, Ephesians 1:5)).

- We have direct access to God through the Holy Spirit (Ephesians 2:18).

- We have been redeemed and forgiven of our sins—not just a few, but *all* of them! (Romans 8:31).

- We have been purchased, bought, and paid for in full (1 Corinthians 6:19-20).

- We are saints, just like Miriam, Deborah, Hannah, Esther, Ruth, Mary, Elizabeth, Anna, Dorcas and all the other amazing women of God in the Bible!

- We have been anointed and sealed by God. That is a permanent seal, stamped on our forehead for the invisible world to see (2 Corinthians 1:21,22).

- God sees us as righteous and holy...*as though we had never sinned, free from condemnation and punishment* (Romans 5:1, 8:1,2).

- We can never be separated from the love of God. It's like two pieces of paper bonded together with Gorilla Glue. One cannot be separated from the other (Romans 8:35).

- We have been given a spirit of power, of love, and of sound mind—spiritual power, selfless love, and a mind that can be victorious over Satan's attacks (2 Timothy 1:7).

- We are now God's family, and Satan cannot touch us without permission from our Father (1 John 5:18).

- We have been chosen and appointed to do good things—things God has planned for us to do (John 15:16).

- We are God's temple—He lives in us, and we need to treat our bodies with the care, respect, and honor we would show God's dwelling place (1 Corinthians 3:16).

- We can approach God with confidence—as confidently as we would approach a loving earthly dad (Ephesians 3:12).

- We can do all things through Christ, who strengthens us—in God's unlimited power, not in our own feeble, failing strength (Philippians 4:13).

Aren't those promises incredible? We are royalty, ladies. We are children of the King...princesses! We have a direct line to the living God who created us, Elohim, the One who can fix everything, provide all things, and enable us to do what we are called to do. And He has promised to never leave us.

But like all relationships, there are two sides. A one-sided relationship lacks substance, therefore God asks a few things of us too. If you feel the Holy Spirit nudging you at any particular point, make a note of it and ask God what He wants you to do in this area.

What are we called to do in this new relationship?

• Submit
James 4:7 *"Submit yourselves, then, to God."*

• Spend time with God
James 4:8 *"Come near to God and He will come near to you."* (Spend daily time in the Bible and prayer.)

• Humble ourselves
James 4:10 *"Humble yourselves before the Lord, and He will lift you up."* (Be honest.)

• Consider it a joy to have trouble, because there is a purpose
James 1:2,3 *"Consider it pure joy, my sisters, whenever you face trials of many kinds, because you know that the testing of your faith produces perseverance."* (We can learn a lot from suffering.)

• Ask for wisdom
James 1:5 *"If any of you lacks wisdom, you should ask of God who gives generously to all without finding fault, and it will be given to you."* (Who doesn't need wisdom?)

• Be messengers
Mark 16:15 *"Go into all the world and preach the gospel."* (Be ready to share your faith.)

• Respect others
James 1:19 *"Be quick to listen, slow to speak, and slow to become angry."* (Yikes!)

• Obey God, and obey His Word
James 1:22 *"Do not merely listen to the Word, but do what it says.*

This verse always brings to mind a powerful memory for me.

When my first two girls were little, I would watch out the door holding my wee son, as they walked hand in hand down the street to school. Heidi was in grade two and Mandi was in kindergarten.

Each morning I noticed another mom walking past with her little girl and a baby in a stroller. One day I felt the Holy Spirit prompting me to ask her in. "Lord!" I said, "I don't even know her!" She walked on past my door, and I breathed a sigh of relief.

The next day as I watched her walk by, my heart quickened as I felt God press me to invite her in for coffee. My excuse was quick. "Oh Lord, I can't today, my house is a mess. I'll ask her tomorrow."

The third day the mother passed my house, I felt a powerful urging to just open the door and start a conversation. But I could not make myself do it. I uttered another weak excuse about needing to do some errands. This time, I did not feel any relief.

The following week, she happened to be there as I stepped out to kiss my girls goodbye. The mom smiled at me. I smiled back. There was no audible voice, but I understood what God wanted. My house was still messy, I still had errands to do, and I still did not know her, but I knew I had to obey. "Hi!" I called. "Would you like to come in for coffee on your way back?"

She smiled deeply and said, "I'd love to!"

Well, that began a wonderful relationship. My new friend ended up coming with me to a Bible study and accepting Jesus into her life. Her husband did too. We kept in touch over the years, rejoicing when their three girls also came to the Lord. One of them married a pastor and they now serve in ministry. How great is God?

God does not always give us several opportunities to obey when He speaks, as He did then. Sometimes when we ignore His voice, the opportunity is gone for good. I will always be grateful I finally chose to open my door so God could show me what happens when we obey His words. That experience will never be forgotten. It changed my walk with God.

• Confess our sins
1 John 1:9 GNB *"If we confess our sins to God, he will keep his promise...He will forgive us our sins and purify us from all wrongdoing."* (When living clean before God is important to us, we will see victory in our life.)

• Repent
I know this may seem similar to confessing sin, but there is an important difference. Confessing is owning up to something, repenting is being genuinely sorry for it. How

often have we said something to one of our kids like, "Say you're sorry to your brother!" and a muted grunt somewhat resembling the word is offered. That is not repenting. There is no true sorrow for the action.

I want you to see a most incredible prayer of repentance from someone we would never think it necessary. Look up Daniel 9:4-18 and read as this man of God pours out his broken heart over the sins of his country, his people, and himself. It convicts and inspires me each time I read it. God honors true repentance and responds in powerful ways. Now read Daniel 9:20-23 and see how God responds to Daniel's prayer.

• Forgive everyone everything (Yup, everything.)
Mark 11:25 GNT *"And when you stand and pray, forgive anything you may have against anyone, so that your Father in heaven will forgive the wrongs you have done."*

This is important. If we have offended anyone, God wants us to make that right. He also wants us to forgive anyone who has hurt us, before we ask for anything from Him.

• Love God with all your heart (More than *anything or anyone* else.)
Deuteronomy 11:13 GNB *"So then obey the commands that I have given you today; love the Lord your God and serve him with all your heart."*

• Serve and sacrifice (We are women, this is what we do!)
Romans 12:1 GNT *"So then, my friends, because of God's great mercy to us, I appeal to you: Offer yourselves as a living sacrifice to God, dedicated to His service and pleasing to Him. This is the true worship you should offer."*

• Thank Him

Psalm 100:4 *"Enter His gates with thanksgiving and His courts with praise; give thanks to Him and praise His name."* (Start each prayer with thanking God for His blessings.)

• Praise Him

This is woven all through Scripture, so we know this is important to God. In some places it seems to open the door of heaven to our requests. In Acts 16 when Paul and Silas were in prison, praying and singing praises, God sent an earthquake to break their chains!

In 2 Chronicles 20:20-26 when the army of Judah was going to war and began singing praises to God, the Lord set an ambush and fought the battle for them, turning those who came against them against each other! When the Judean army arrived at the battlefield, dead bodies of their enemies covered the ground.

Praise and worship are mighty weapons against the devil and an act of obedience that brings the blessing of God.

Psalm 100:1 *"Shout for joy to the Lord, all the earth. Worship the Lord with gladness; come before him with joyful songs."*

Praise is important to God. If you run out of things to praise Him for, sing a song or read a psalm out loud.

• Proclaim the good news (We can start with our kids and family.)

Matthew 28:18 *"Then Jesus came to them and said, 'All authority in heaven and on earth has been given to me. Therefore go and make disciples of all nations, baptizing them in the name of the Father and of the Son and of the Holy Spirit,* and *teach them to obey everything I have commanded you'''* (emphasis added).

- **Drive out demons and pray for healing** (Yes! We'll learn more about this, and how to do it boldly in the name of Jesus.)
Luke 9:1 *"When Jesus had called the twelve together, he gave them power and authority to drive out all demons and to cure diseases."*

- **Be strong!** (If we are old, weak or sick, we can still be strong in spirit.)
Ephesians 6:10 *"Finally, be strong in the Lord and in his mighty power."*

- **Fight the enemy!** (Never give up.)
Ephesians 6:12 *"For our struggle is not against flesh and blood, but against the rulers, against the authorities, against the powers of this dark world, and against the spiritual forces of evil in the heavenly realm."*

* Fast and pray

Scripture reveals so many that have been called to fast to see the hand of God in either salvation, healing, or an answer to prayer. Queen Esther fasted for the salvation of her people, (1Kings 4:16), David fasted for the healing of his baby, (2Samuel 12:16), Daniel fasted for an answer to prayer, (Daniel 10:3), Nehemiah fasted to see God's forgiveness for the Israelites, (Nehemiah 1:4), Joel fasted in obedience to God, (2:12), Anna, the prophetess fasted for the coming of the messiah, (Luke 2:37), and *Jesus* fasted in preparation to face the temptation of Satan, (Luke 4:2).

If Jesus felt He needed to fast, why would we not think it's something we should do?

Jesus said in Matthew 6:17,18 *"When you fast, put oil on your head and wash your face, so that it will not be obvious to others that you are fasting, but only to your Father, who is unseen; and your Father, who sees what is done in secret, will reward you."*

Did you notice that first word...when. Jesus did not say if, He said when. Fasting is something we are all called to at different times for different reasons. One week, one day, one meal, one coffee...just give up something and use that hunger pain to remind you to pray. God will make the time for fasting clear, all we have to do is obey. (We will learn more about this in chapter twelve.)

- **Get dressed and take a stand** (The wardrobe He gives always fits us perfectly.
  Ephesians 6:13 *"Therefore put on the full armor of God, so that when the day of evil comes, you may be able to stand your ground, and after you have done everything, to stand."*

- **Be filled with the Spirit**
Years ago this seemed an impossible challenge to me. I didn't know how to go about it, and the things I heard from my charismatic friends seemed a little intimidating. I pictured myself awkwardly standing at a slightly open door, feebly motioning to some invisible entity to come. Come on in. Take your shoes off and set a spell. But wasn't sure how to know if the welcomed guest had accepted my invitation, or if He would be uncomfortable in me and leave. It took searching the scriptures, deep cleansing prayer, and making the choice to believe God's Word to gain understanding.

What I learned was that the moment I became a Christian, the Holy Spirit came to dwell in me. He was there to stay until I left this world and moved to heaven. I learned He is there for many purposes: comforter, conscience tweaker, truth revealer, sin exposer, teacher, reminder, promise filler, guarantor, protector, and much more.

I also learned the Holy Spirit takes up whatever space in my heart I give Him. If I allow myself, or Satan, room, the Holy Spirit has less. Consistently asking God to search my heart and deal with any sin gives the Holy Spirit more control. The more yielded I am to His will, the more power of God I will see in my life.

Shockingly, I found it possible to feel filled with the Spirit of God one moment and, perhaps an hour later, spew vile words at my husband, children, or some faceless, annoying telemarketer. Somehow, that filling of the Spirit leaked, and my old nature seeped into the space, embarrassing me with my own behavior. I quickly found choosing to live in the power of the Holy Spirit is not a one-time deal—it is a practice and a discipline. Some days it is every hour on the hour, but it did get easier with diligence. God's holiness slowly became a constant part of my thoughts, actions, and decisions. The journey has become clear and comfortable, a continuing practice of God's presence.

Ephesians 1:13 *"Having believed, you were marked in Him with a seal, the promised Holy Spirit, who is a deposit guaranteeing our inheritance until the redemption of those who are God's possession."*

We'll be looking more closely at this in later chapters. So don't quit here, its going to be good!

Questions

Have you ever felt the hopelessness Lovely felt in her story? Can you journal about that time?

List five things God has promised for us when we give Him our heart and life.

Which of our identities from the list speak most powerfully to you? Why?

What do you think about God calling you His perfect workmanship, royalty, chosen, and appointed? Does this make a difference in how you see yourself? How can it make a difference in your choices?

What would be the hardest thing for you to do from the list of God's calling? Which would be the easiest? Take a moment to ask the Holy Spirit to help you implement these things into your life, and to niggle your conscience when you forget.

Chapter Four
Satan's Sad Story

It was midnight, and the dark figure slipped silently through the shifting shadows, making his way back to the girl's shack. The full moon shed light on his path, and he glanced down at his double shadow. He grinned in acknowledgment of the evil spirits that traveled with him. "How dare that girl tell me about her God! Me, a great sorcerer! She thinks her Jesus is protecting her? I'll show her some Jesus. My master is greater than hers. I'll turn her into a donkey to ride around town before I end her life!"

Standing in front of the small hut, he softly chanted a few mystic words and watched the locked door swing open. Moving to her cot where she slept, he quietly shifted his leg to straddle her slight body and cast the curse. As his leg brushed against her, a sudden powerful thrust threw him onto the floor, knocking the wind from his lungs and crumpling his legs beneath him.

He groaned with the pain, but demonic voices screamed in his head to keep trying. He pulled himself off the floor for another attempt. This time he would be successful! Carefully raising his leg over her, he held his breath until he felt his foot touch the other side. Immediately, with a vicious force, swift and strong, the witch doctor was picked up, hurled to the ground, then pinned by an invisible hand. Evil spirits quickly fled as the new force claimed control. The powerful sorcerer who had held a reign of terror over Haiti for so many years now lay helpless in a splayed heap on the dirt floor of a shabby hut, broken, beaten, and paralyzed. "Where is my master Satan, and why have I no powers?" he whimpered. "And who holds me prisoner?" *Could it possibly be her God*?[5]

This excerpt from *Acting Badly* is about a man known as Agi Mal, a powerful Haitian witch doctor who served Satan for sixty-two years but met Jesus on what he called his "road to Damascus" experience. Satan's despicable nature and his limitations are glaringly evident throughout this story. Agi Mal knew his master Lucifer was very strong, always giving him great magic, but he was not prepared for meeting the living God and the ensuing journey that led to his redemption. I was privileged to know Agi Mal and hear his story firsthand. It opened my eyes in a greater way and taught me things about the invisible world I could not otherwise know.

There are many other stories of people redeemed out of Satanism and devil worship, even in North America. From these personal experiences, we learn a lot about this entity often referred to as "the enemy." In John 10:10 we learn the thief, Satan, has come only to steal, kill and destroy. His goal is to steal our peace and joy, to kill our bodies, and to destroy our faith, our future, and our relationships!

We need to know all we can about this evil being, and the best place to do our research is always Scripture, where we learn Satan's beginnings, his purpose, his plan, his fall, and his destiny. Let's see what God reveals!

---

[5] Heather Rodin, *Acting Badly: A Sorcerer's Story of Redemption*. Word Alive Press, 2017.

According to Ezekiel 28, Lucifer was the seal of perfection, full of wisdom, perfect in beauty—an anointed guardian cherub. His job was to cover the place with his wings where God's glory would manifest. He was made powerful, radiant, wise, and glorious—a reflection of God's beauty.

But Lucifer is also a created being. God created him, and he has all the limitations of one created. Although powerful, Satan has always been and always will be under the control of the living God.

If his purpose was to reflect and protect the glory of God, what in heaven happened?

Pride happened. Lucifer was so impressed with his own beauty, intelligence, and position, he wanted more. He wanted to be like God. Well, to *be* God actually, so he caused an insurrection in heaven to overthrow God. Satan wanted the glory that he was created to protect. Pride and arrogance was the beginning of sin.

In Proverbs 16:18 we read, *"Pride goes before destruction, and a haughty spirit before a fall."* And fall was exactly what Lucifer did. But there was more.

Defiance. His attitude was one of rebellion. Isaiah 14:13, 14 NKJV refers to Satan's defiance. *"You have said in your heart: 'I will ascend into heaven. I will exalt my throne above the stars of God; I will also sit on the mount of the congregation...I will ascend above the heights of the clouds, I will be like the Most High.'"*

Five times Satan said, "I will" with no thought of God's will. (Can we relate to that?)

The five *I wills* of Satan were spat in God's face, and as a result, God brought him down along with the angels he had convinced to throw their vote his way.

The devil and his following were tossed to earth, and his name was changed from Lucifer, which means, "to shine," to Satan, which means "adversary."

An adversary is one who is on the attack, an enemy, a foe, or a rival. An opponent. How fitting. Satan not only opposes God and anything God has created but also continually attacks His kingdom—especially anyone who belongs to that kingdom: believers, followers of Jesus, Christians.

God could have sent Lucifer straight to hell, but instead He chose to use him—perhaps to demonstrate truths that would have remained hidden if evil had not entered this world. Maybe truths about ourselves and our inner penchant for evil, selfish desires, injustice, self-pity, and rebellion. But although he remains active for a time, Satan cannot act without God's permission.

Dr. Erwin Lutzer, Pastor Emeritus of Moody Church, says, "The devil is God's devil, and is being used to play an important part in God's unfolding plan."[6]

God is not afraid of Satan and maintains control over him, as we see in the book of Job when Satan stood in front of God and asked permission to attack the man of God, supposedly to prove that people only serve God when things are going well. God allowed it, with stipulations, and that incredible story has helped people through the ages deal with difficulties, and still trust in God.

---

[6] Dr. Erwin Lutzer, *God's Devil.* Moody Publishers, 2015.

I want this to be clear: God is on His throne. He rules over kings, queens, presidents, prime ministers, dictators, oligarchs, world leaders, and heads of state and organizations. He is not only our God, He is Satan's God and is in complete control of him. God uses all things to work out His will and plan for His creation. So if God is not wringing His hands and wondering what to do, we shouldn't either.

What does Satan want?

That is a simple question to answer. Satan is so obvious. He wants us to sin. He wants us to reject God. He wants us to ignore Jesus. He wants us to rebel. He wants to ruin our families. He wants us miserable. He wants us sick. He wants us dead. He wants us to go to hell. Remember John 10:10? *"The thief has come to steal, kill, and destroy."*

For reasons only God knows, Satan was allowed to keep an amount of power for a time, with occasional access to heaven and God's presence (Job 1:6-12, Ezekiel 28:11, Zechariah 3:1,2). Yet his lofty and unfulfilled goal of being a powerful ruler remains. He thinks he rules a kingdom, but in reality, God rules that too. People think he rules hell, but Satan does not rule anything. His freedom is only as great as God allows. Satan's plans are of darkness, evil, death, destruction, and devastation, but God holds all things in His hands and we can trust in that truth and "fear not"!

In the Garden of Eden, the enemy exerted all his efforts to destroy the relationship Adam and Eve had with the Father. He thought if he could just get them to sin, it would be a great victory for him—he would gain authority over them. So He encouraged the same two sins with Adam and Eve that had caused his own fall—pride and defiance. Satan took on a serpent form, slithered over and whispered to

Eve that God wanted to keep them from something good, coaxing them to rebel by eating the forbidden fruit. He told them they would be greater, smarter, and more powerful than God if they ate the fruit. And eat it they did. Eve took a bite, decided it tasted good, turned to her husband standing silently beside her, and gave the fruit to him. He also took a bite, knowing full well God had forbidden this very action.

That act of rebellion brought about the fall of mankind, changing the hierarchy of power in the spirit realm to give Satan an allotment of authority over us.

Centuries of Satan's wretched reign over the earth and the ensuing sins of man are recorded down through history and throughout Scripture. But God cannot tolerate sin, and sin had to be paid for. The punishment was a required sacrifice. Only one without sin could be that sacrifice. But no one was sinless. There was no one who could be the perfect sacrifice for all. The animal blood sacrifices in the Old Testament were a temporary solution God so graciously gave, but He had a plan for a better way, a permanent payment.

God put His plan into action and sent His perfect Son Jesus—who had never sinned—to be born as a human. He would live, teach, suffer loss and betrayal, be tempted, and ultimately give up His life to be the otherwise unattainable sacrifice for our sins. His death would be violent, painful, and horrific. But He did it willingly, covering our sins with His shed blood. Thank goodness that was not the end.

He rose from the dead, leaving the tomb as empty as it was before He was laid there. He was seen by many, shared a meal with His disciples, then in front of a mass of spectators ascended into heaven to prepare a place for us! Jesus Christ defeated sin and death.

That changed everything!

At Christ's crucifixion, His burial, and His resurrection, the adversary was defeated completely and he immediately lost authority over believers. Lucifer and his dark angels were relegated to the bottom rung of authority.

The devil knows he has been stripped of his power over God's people. But he also knows most of us are uninformed about our victory, so he continues to manipulate and destroy lives and relationships as we ignorantly allow him access. If Satan is not challenged, bound, and cast from this goal of his, he will continue. If we don't understand what the death of Jesus has done for us, and the authority that has been given back to us, he will take total advantage and keep tormenting us. If we do not step up and accept the gift made available through God's incredible sacrifice, the enemy will hound and oppress us. Failing to recognize his calling card, we unwittingly allow him to usurp control in our lives—control that rightly belongs to God.

Jesus did not die on the cross only to forgive our sins and give us eternal life, He also died on the cross to give us abundant life—now! Jesus conquered the grave, but He also conquered Satan, and wants us to live in that victory He won.

It is up to us to learn how to identify his presence and his handiwork, take the authority Jesus won back for us, and deal with this beaten, already conquered evil.

Luke 10:17,18 *"The seventy-two returned with joy and said, 'Lord, even the demons submit to us in Your name.' Jesus replied, 'I saw Satan fall like lightning from heaven. I have given you authority to trample on snakes and scorpions and to overcome all the power of the enemy; nothing will harm you. However, do not rejoice that the spirits submit to you, but rejoice that your names are written in heaven.'"*

We shall see in later chapters that having authority to bind and cast the devil from our lives and those of our children is an amazing gift. But we need to be careful and not think it's because of anything we've done or in our own power. It is *only* in the power of the name of Jesus *"that every knee shall bow, in heaven, on earth, and under the earth"* (Philippians 2:10), and that includes the demonic world. We can do nothing in and of ourselves, but *"we can do all things through Christ who strengthens us"* (Philippians 4:13).

What about Satan's kingdom?

Satan is always trying to be like his creator, God. He is the great counterfeiter and attempts to have his dark kingdom reflect God's holy one. The empire of evil is listed in Ephesians 6:12 as "rulers, authorities, powers, and spiritual forces of evil." The *rulers* are believed to be over countries and *authorities* are over districts, areas, and bodies of water. These two are the most powerful demonic beings. *Powers* are demons in special places, and *spiritual forces of evil* are the multitude of demons working for Satan worshippers, witches, mediums, and sorcerers. All seek influence over humans all the time!

We read in Daniel chapter nine of a powerful cherubim bringing an answer to Daniel's prayer. The angel told Daniel that his prayer had been heard as it was being prayed but that the "Prince of Persia" had held up the answer for three weeks! It wasn't until Michael, the warrior archangel, came to the rescue and took over the fight that the message could be delivered. It's believed the Prince of Persia was a powerful spirit in Satan's kingdom. A great thing learned from this story is that God's army is stronger than Satan's and will ultimately win the battles fought in the heavenly realms. Although our prayers are always heard, their answer, like Daniel's, may be held up. The answers to our prayers will come, but in God's perfect time.

Sadly, Satan has been given some power not only over his kingdom of fallen angels, but also over people who have not accepted Jesus as Savior. His power over believers is limited to what God allows to fulfill His purposes. Sorcerers in Satan worship believe the souls of unbelievers that have died without accepting Christ are still under the control of Satan until the great judgment. Scripture does not qualify this concept that I have seen, but what a disconcerting thought!

So what's Satan's plan?

He wants to distort the gospel and render believers useless, hopeless, and worthless. We are the prize, the trophy, the gilded treasure. That battle will rage between heaven and hell until Jesus returns, the Alpha and the Omega, the First and the Last, the Beginning and the End.

Satan is not happy when Christians find joy and peace in Jesus and enjoy time with other Christians, because he has nothing to offer that can compete. So if he can get us to neglect fellowship with other believers, neglect our devotional time each day, miss church, and stop praying, that will weaken us, and there's a greater chance we will become discouraged and distracted and lose faith. Satan wants to bring us into despair. He wants us to commit a sin that discredits our testimony. He wants us to turn away from the will of God, the Word of God, and the cross of His Son. Then he will have us right where he wants us!

Acts 13:9,10 *"Then Saul, who was called Paul, filled with the Holy Spirit, looked straight at Elymas (a sorcerer) and said, 'You are a child of the devil and an enemy of everything that is right! You are full of all kinds of deceit and trickery. Will you never stop perverting the right ways of the Lord?'"*

What is Satan's destiny?

Satan is eventually to be cast into the lake of fire for all eternity. Here are a few things we learn about hell from Scripture.

- God prepared hell for creatures doomed to spend eternity there.
- Hell is referred to as the lake of fire, a place of torment.
- Hell is eternal.
- Hell is just.

Revelation 20:10 *"And the devil who had deceived them was thrown into the lake of fire and sulfur where the beast and the false prophet were, and they will be tormented day and night forever and ever."*

There is coming a day when this evil entity will no longer be a problem, but for now, we need to learn how to identify the strategies he uses to coax us into sin, and keep us from experiencing God's abundant life.

His strategies are identifiable—and in the next chapter we will see some strong ones; perhaps a few you have already experienced in your own life.

To learn more about the names of Satan and what demons are like, see Appendix B at the end of the book.

So keep going! Satan will loose power over you as his plans are exposed and God's power is revealed. The secrets to finding freedom are becoming clear.

Questions

Does learning about Satan's power shock you? Write a sentence describing how you have viewed him in the past, and another about how you view him now.

What was the main sin that brought Satan down? Have you ever noticed pride and arrogance in your own life? How has learning God's view of that affected you?

In the Garden of Eden, Satan used the tools of confusion and doubt on Eve. Describe a time in your life when he used those tools on you. What were the consequences?

How does seeing the answer to Daniel's prayer being held up by demonic forces, and being freed by angelic beings, give some clarity to issues of unanswered prayers in your life? In what way does it change things for you?

Have you ever thought of Satan as a roaring lion seeking ways to get to you?

The Lord's Prayer includes praying for deliverance from evil. How will you implement that in your own life?

Read James 2:19. Do you see the difference between believing there is a God and believing in God?

Is there a special take-away for you from this chapter?

Chapter Five
The Serpent's Strategies

We're learning Satan's plans to gain a place in our life. That is called a stronghold. The simple definition of a spiritual stronghold is a "belief, feeling or desire contrary to the will of God" or a "powerful grip on us by another." It's what 2 Corinthians 10:4-6 refers to as a pretention (warped philosophy) set against the knowledge of God. Think of it as a lie against God's truth that has set in like a fresh perm! The longer it is allowed to stay, the kinkier is gets and the harder it will be to straighten out.

The list of Satan's dirty tricks is long. We need to be aware of as many as possible in order to stop them before they gain any ground in our life and royally mess us up!

I'm going to slip in a confession here. I've seldom stood before the mirror while wearing my glasses! It's horrifying to see the aging process stalking my face, so I preferred to remain in denial. The problem was, as long as I was blind to that issue, I was also blind to another—and one day that issue surfaced.

I'd forgotten I had glasses on and went to the bathroom to start the regular morning process of scrubbing, toning, and lathering on the extra moisturizing-wrinkle removing-skin-perfecting cream. As I looked away from the mirror, my eyes fell to the sink before me. I was appalled! The sink was a mess! Because of my self-imposed blindness, I had not seen the dirt, hair, and toothpaste taking up residence in my sink. I do a good clean on Saturdays and always figured that was enough, but obviously not. If I had not put on my glasses that morning, I would have continued living in an unnecessary, unhealthy situation. Grabbing the bathroom cleaner close at hand, I began to clean, scrub, and rinse until the sink glistened a bright white.

That story, although perhaps shocking to many of you, and I apologize for that, holds a spiritual lesson.

God waits for us to put on our spiritual glasses and take a good look at the mess we've allowed to build within us. He wants His Holy Spirit (who is also close at hand) to be our "cleanser" and scrub us clean, brilliant and glowing in our freedom from sin. And He wants to keep us that way as we start each day whispering that request. It is a game-changing strategy! Starting the day with Jesus is a key to the secret of His presence as we slip into our daily regimen.

Just as I now put on those glasses every morning so I can start the day with a clean sink, I then pick up my Bible so I can start the day with a clean heart.

But let's get into the raw truth of how that old serpent seeks to destroy us, so we can arm ourselves against it.

• Create the fear of death

The horrors of suicide and thoughts of self-harm are incredibly prominent in our society. How can this be in a country with such affluence and abundance? There is seldom anything we cannot access or achieve, so why this overwhelming oppression? Why is the thought of death more enticing than living? Scripture tells us the answer to that question. Satan's goal is to render us useless to the kingdom of God. He wants us gone and dead, and his evil minions work very hard at keeping us so consumed with failure, hopelessness, and depression that our minds look to death as freedom from this torment. If we can recognize

Satan's signature when it scratches our thoughts, we can take them to God and trust Him with our anguish. He will walk through the dark valley with us, leading us to a place of peace.

1 Peter 5:8 *"Be alert and of sober mind. Your enemy the devil prowls around like a roaring lion, looking for someone to devour."*

• Cause Christians to stumble

2 Timothy 2:24-26 MSG *"God's servant must not be argumentative, but a gentle listener and a teacher who keeps cool, working firmly but patiently with those who refuse to obey. You never know how or when God might sober them up with a change of heart and a turning to the truth, enabling them to escape the devil's trap, where they are caught and held captive, forced to run his errands."*

Satan wants to force us to run his errands? We know enough about him to realize these are not good, wholesome things he has in mind. They will be hurtful, disrespectful, demeaning, and downright sinful. He wants us to wreak havoc in our own lives and those of others with our words, our thoughts, and our actions. Let's beware of his tactics and infiltration.

• Blind minds to the truth

It is not known who wrote the book of Hebrews, but Priscilla has been suggested as a possible candidate. I like to think God used a woman to contribute to His holy Word. But whoever the author, we see abundant encouragement in chapter 12, verse 2, to fix our eyes on Jesus and on His truth. When we do this, it says, we will not grow weary and lose heart! Satan hates when we keep our eyes on Jesus because it diminishes his power over us.

2 Corinthians 4:4 *"The god of this age has blinded the minds of unbelievers, so that they cannot see the light of the gospel that displays the glory of Christ, who is the image of God."*

• Imitate true religion and introduce false religion

Satan loves to make us think we are religious even while causing us to question God. He attempts to pull us into false religions that diminish the supreme power of Almighty God, cause us to question the validity of the Bible, draw our eyes from humility to focus on humanism, and slowly turn our hearts from the one true God to accept other gods such as pseudo-science, skepticism, and self-importance.

2 Corinthians 11:14 *"And no wonder, for Satan himself masquerades as an angel of light."*

• Misuse Scripture to confuse

In the temptation of Christ, Satan actually used Scripture to attempt to cause Jesus to sin. He arrogantly recited Psalm 91:11. *"If you are the Son of God, throw Yourself down. For it is written, He [God] will command His angels concerning You, and they will lift You up in their hands so that You will not strike Your foot against a stone."*

Satan used this Scripture in attempt to convince Jesus to obey *him*, therefore not obeying the Father, and ultimately sin! If Satan had been successful, Jesus would no longer be the perfect sacrifice and there would have been no hope for any of us!

• Imitate signs and wonders to distract and offer occult alternatives

We see in the story of Moses and Aaron, appearing before Pharaoh in Exodus 7:8-13, that the court sorcerers and magicians were able to replicate their initial miracle. Satan is powerful and is able to do many miraculous things, but as we see in this story, God is still greater. No matter how Satan distracts with signs and wonders, God will only allow them when it serves a purpose. We must be careful not to rely on miracles alone, but let the Word of God be the basis of our faith.

Mark 13:22 *"For false messiahs and false prophets will appear and perform signs and wonders to deceive, if possible, even the elect."* (We are the elect.)

Seeking guidance through a medium, a sorcerer, tarot cards, palm reading, Ouija boards, or horoscopes is actually calling on a demonic source to give us guidance. This is usually the beginning of satanic oppression in our lives that can bring with it a host of troubles. The spirit of witchcraft opens us to a world of evil, and God forbids it!

Deuteronomy 18:9-12 (MSG) *"...Don't practice divination, sorcery, fortunetelling, witchery, casting spells, holding séances, or channeling with the dead. People who do these things are an abomination to God."*

• Destroy faith

The Apostle Paul wrote in 2 Corinthians 11:3, *"But I am afraid that just as Eve was deceived by the serpent's cunning, your minds may somehow be led astray from your sincere and pure devotion to Christ."*

Jesus told the story of the sower of seeds in Matthew 13, a parable reflecting the gospel and how it is received. In this story, the farmer scatters the seed (the gospel) but three things keep them from growing.

First, seeds fall on rocky soil. This could involve Satan's arguments, perhaps scientific or theological, introducing skepticism to keep belief at bay. Then Satan quickly snatches away the words of God so they cannot take root.

Second was a scorching sun that shriveled and dried up little sprouts of faith. This represents a lack of character, responding to the gospel emotionally. Emotions soon wear off, and people are back to where they started before hearing the gospel.

Third, thorns grow up and choke the promising new plants. Perhaps this refers to addictions, problems, sickness, worry, no immediate answer to a prayer, wanting freedom from moral rightness to follow selfish desires, or a powerful draw back into a sin that silences the words of God.

Satan works hard at using one or all of these blockades to prevent salvation.

• Bring sickness to discourage

In Job 1:6, Satan appeared before the Father in heaven and God asked him where he had been. He responded saying, "I was roaming the earth." God asked him if he had seen His servant Job, a blameless and upright man who feared God and shunned evil. Satan got his hackles up and accused God of making things so good for Job and blessing him with special protection that Job didn't need to look elsewhere. Let's listen in on that conversation.

In Job 1:9, Satan replied, "'*Does Job fear God for nothing? Have you not put a hedge around him, his household and everything he has? You have blessed the work of his hands, so that his flocks and herds are spread through the land. But now stretch out your hand and strike everything he has, and he will surely curse you to your face.' The Lord said to Satan, 'Very well, then, everything he has is in your power, but on the man himself do not lay a finger.'*"

Satan then did a number on Job. He had his oxen and donkeys stolen and servants killed, he burned up the sheep and shepherds, had his camel herd stolen, and killed his ten children.

Job's response was to tear his robes, shave his head, then fall to the ground and worship God. Weeping, Job cried out, "*Naked I came from my mother's womb, and naked I will depart. The Lord gave and the Lord has taken away; may the name of the Lord be praised*" (Job 1:20,21).

Job did not sin, and Satan was miffed. Now he really wanted to kill Job. The conversation continued.

Job 2:3b,4,5 "*Then the Lord said to Satan, 'There is no one on earth like Job; he is blameless and upright, a man who fears God and shuns evil. And he still maintains his integrity, though you incited me against him to ruin him without any reason.'*

"'*Skin for skin!' Satan replied. 'A man will give all he has for his own life. But now stretch out Your hand and strike his flesh and bones and he will surely curse you to your face.'*

"*The Lord said to Satan, 'Very well then, he is in your hands; but you must spare his life.'*"

Satan took that permission and ran with it, horribly disfiguring Job with ugly boils and sores from the soles of his feet to the top of his recently shaved head. The rest of the story is wonderful reading, but here is the Coles notes version: Job's friends came and heaped judgment on him, trying to make him feel all this had come as punishment from God. But at the end of chapter 42, after Job had prayed for his friends, God restored more to him than he had before, including children. Job lived to 140 years and died a wealthy, happy, godly, fulfilled man.

Satan had tried to use sickness and sorrow to beat out Job's faith, but he lost. Neither should we give him victory over us in times of pain and sorrow.

• Cause dissension among believers and families

Discord, strife, contention, and disagreements surround us every day. Church life and relationships with other Christians are not immune to these struggles. These issues are often covertly disguised as understandable complications and are tolerated as part of being human, but Satan is quick to jump in and stir the pot until a small argument becomes a major division in the ranks. Paul instructs us in Ephesians 4:6, *"In your anger do not sin. Do not let the sun go down while you are still angry, and do not give the devil a foothold."* Dissension is Satan's strategy here.

Romans 16:17-20 *"I urge you, brothers and sisters, to watch out for those who cause divisions and put obstacles in your way that are contrary to the teaching you have learned. Keep away from them. For such people are not serving our Lord Christ, but their own appetites. By smooth talk and flattery they deceive the minds of naive people. Everyone has heard about your obedience, so I rejoice because of you; but I want* you to be wise about what is good and innocent, and about what is evil. The God of peace will soon crush Satan under your feet."

• Tempt with sexual allurement

Today's society has an epidemic of pornography addiction, sex trafficking, and infidelity in marriage, perversion, and sexual abuse. Children are now sexually active at extremely young ages and presenting sexually transmitted diseases that only a few years ago were seldom seen in adults. As early in recorded history as Genesis chapter 12, we see Satan using sex as a gateway to sin. Now it pervades everything from television shows to movies to best selling books to what has become an acceptable, normal lifestyle.

1 Thessalonians 4:3-5 *"It is God's will that you should be sanctified: that you should avoid sexual immorality; that each of you should learn to control his own body in a way that is holy and honorable..."*

• Instill rage and anger

We will cover this a little farther on in the book, but we need to see that Satan is often behind it. We see this even in our young children—exploding rage when things aren't going their way. We look at them, at our spouse, and at ourselves in the mirror when tantrums happen, wondering where it comes from. It has become so prevalent this now has a clinical diagnosis as "oppositional defiant disorder."

Uncontrolled anger can do a lot of damage in relationships. Apologies are great, but often the damage done is hard to undo.

Proverbs 29:22 *"An angry [woman] stirs up dissension, and a hot-tempered one commits many sins."*

• Establish pride that leads to a fall

Pride is so easy to excuse. We can call it self-assurance, self-confidence, courage, tenacity, independence, self-reliance, or a type-A personality. All those things are admired by society and sought after in business. But there is a fine line that bleeds into pride and arrogance, which God sees as sin. Self-sufficiency says, "I have done great things, I am doing fine on my own, and I am to be celebrated." This is self-worship. When we inadvertently worship ourselves, we steal worship that should be God's. That is idol worship, and God forbids it. It is also what brought about the fall of Lucifer. Pride will always bring us down in the end.

Philippians 2:3 *"Do nothing out of selfish ambition or vain conceit, but in humility consider others better than yourselves."*

These are just a few ways Satan attempts to conquer us, and I trust this helps to identify his tactics. We know that *anything turning us away* from our faith, from our desire to be in God's Word, from being with other Christians, or from a growing relationship with Jesus is not from God. It's from Satan. As we are able to recognize the enemy's infiltration, we are better able to counter-attack!

How does the devil work?

He lies
John 8:44 *"You belong to your father, the devil, and you want to carry out your father's desires. He was a murderer from the beginning, not holding to the truth, for there is no truth in him."*

He is a tempter
Matthew 4:3 *"Then Jesus was led by the Spirit into the wilderness to be tempted by the devil. After fasting forty days and forty nights, he was hungry. The tempter came to Him and said, 'If you are the Son of God, tell these stones to become bread.'"*

This whole passage is worth reading to see all the ways Satan tempted God's Son and how Jesus rebuked him. But if Satan is not afraid to tempt Jesus, he is certainly not going to shy away from tempting us! Just as Jesus used Scripture to deal with the enemy, so should we. We can also command the evil one, in the powerful name of Jesus, to leave us alone.

He is the accuser of the believer
Revelation 12:10 *"Then I heard a loud voice in heaven say: Now have come the salvation and the power and the kingdom of our God and the authority of his Messiah. For the accuser of our brothers and sisters, who accuses them before our God day and night, has been hurled down."*

Every time we sin, we give Satan an occasion to go before God and point his evil, bent finger at us saying, "Look at your child. She is failing you again. Why don't you just let me remove her from the earth?"

Jesus must smile at his fury, reminding him that when He died on the cross, it was for those sins. His shed blood covers us, as though we have never sinned. Satan may see our failures, but when God looks at us, He only sees His Son's righteousness, and there is no judgment upon us. Satan then has to leave God's presence, dissatisfied once again.

Neil Anderson deals with this issue in his book *The Bondage Breaker* (which I encourage everyone to read).[7] In it he offers a very long list to deal with, in order to live the abundant life God wants for us. I've used some of his and added several more in the column below. I'm now asking you to take your time and pray through them all, allowing specific issues that need to go, be identified. Dealing with each, repenting and renouncing one at a time, weakens Satan's control over us, and the burdens slowly fall away. Taking the authority God provides to rebuke the devil in the name of Jesus, releases his grip on our life, and allows us to move on in freedom.

Grab your spiritual glasses, and prayerfully read through the list. Circle the ones you feel have a grip on your life and must be dealt with.

- addiction to social media
- addiction to your cell phone or other device
- obsessions (news/political/trending)
- jealousy/envy
- pride and arrogance
- sarcasm
- fighting, quarreling, yelling
- complaining

---

[7] Neil Anderson, *The Bondage Breaker.* Harvest House, 2000.

- criticism/critical spirit
- gossip/rumors
- apathy/laziness
- hatred/resentment/offense
- physical hurt from abuse
  and emotional wounds from abuse
- bitterness
- trauma (physical/emotional)
- cheating
- materialism/greed
- stealing
- shopping/spending addiction
- language (swearing/cussing/foul)
- lying
- anger/rage
- excessiveness in any area
- procrastination
- eating disorders (too much/too little)
- substance abuse (drugs/alcohol/soft drinks/caffeine/ sugar)
- thoughts of death
- suicidal tendencies
- perfectionism
- discontentment
- ignorance and spiritual disinterest
- self-pity
- selfish ambition
- sexual sins
- immorality (past/present)
- boasting/bragging
- scoffing/mockery
- always comparing yourself to others
- generational sins (abuse/addiction/self-harm/rage/ critical spirit, etc.)
- unforgiveness toward another (warranted or not)

- idolatry (putting *anything* before your relationship with Jesus)
- witchcraft/rebellion (seen as the same thing), evil practices, divination

As you read through those issues, I'm pretty sure pictures popped into your head of your husband, your kids, someone else's kids, your mother-in-law, a difficult neighbor, an ex-husband, someone at church, someone in your past, a parent, or a sibling. It is easy to read those things and see others.

But *now* I want you to go back through it more slowly. Don't hurry, and don't skip over some you may want to discard as not important. I want you to stop at each one and ask God if that is in you. If you have complete peace that it is not, move on. But if you find yourself under the slightest bit of conviction, circle it and take a few moments to confess it to God. Ask Him to reveal whatever instances in your life need to be confronted, confessed, and renounced. As God brings remembrances to mind, do it right there and then. After dealing with it, go on to the next one and do the same.

You have just unlocked a secret in spiritual warfare. Tuck that key away to be used again whenever God prompts you.

Don't be surprised if this process is not done in an hour, a day, or even a week. Many of these things will have become deeply ingrained, habits so embedded in our life they'll keep showing up. It may take dedicated, concerted effort to break free, but don't give up. Once you get started, God can keep bringing things to mind you have not thought about in years! (I know He has done that for me.) Each time you confess that as sin and renounce it (deny it a place), a deeper healing takes place. Then ask the Holy Spirit to fill the space vacated.

Two things are going to happen. First you'll start to recognize struggles more quickly that God reveals because you are more in tune with the Holy Spirit, and second, this will happen less and less as God is given more space in your life and Satan is squeezed out.

If you are like me, you've ended up with quite a few in that list to circle. I often dismissed these issues as shortcomings, habits, or inherited faults. And I was right, but I needed to look deeper to see them as God sees them—sin. I know now what can begin as something small can be used by Satan to develop into a compulsive behavior that pushes the Holy Spirit out of a place of control and gives himself an opportunity to dig in and establish a presence. That toehold becomes a foothold, then the foothold becomes a stronghold, and that stronghold will affect everything we think and do in a dark and negative way.

Look at it this way.

When food boils over on the stove and I don't clean it up right away, then more food boils over time and time again, it becomes a big problem—a burnt on, rock hard, difficult-to-deal-with disaster. It is going to take some serious time and intentional scraping to restore that grunge back to a clean surface. But if I scrub if off every time it happens, it's easier to deal with when it happens again, and the stove remains clean.

In the same manner, when we have sin in our life and we do not deal with it right away, it becomes a burnt-on, rock-hard problem and requires a time of repentance, renouncing, and the cleansing work of the Holy Spirit to get rid of the filth and leave us with a fragrance of clean before the Lord. Regularly dealing with head and heart issues as we recognize them keeps Jesus in control and the enemy from gaining ground.

Gord and I have a small garden in front of our garage. I've walked past it every day for years. In the past, I would stoop and pull out a few obvious weeds on my way to the car, but those pesky little ones just kept growing bigger and spreading furtively. I never really got control over them. Each time I looked at it, I was disgusted. My half-hearted effort never resulted in the lovely, weed-free garden I desired. I gave up.

This year, Gord said he'd had enough, took an entire day off, and did it right. He pulled up *every* weed by the deep roots, put down a weed-block cloth that covered the dirt and tucked it around our Annabelle hydrangea plants, spread rich, black bark mulch, and watered it well. There has not been a weed all summer. That little strip of garden is a pleasure to behold. If only he had done the work sooner, there would have been less disappointment and more joy when I walked by that garden! Haha, just kidding! I probably should have risen to that challenge.

I'm sure you know where I'm going with this and see the application, but I'll say it anyways. We often tolerate pesky little sins, and like those weeds, they bug us, but we get used to them. It takes the Holy Spirit's prompting and conviction for us to deal with them. But taking time to confront those sins every time they rear their ugly heads (just as you have done earlier in this chapter), results in freedom, joy, and blessing. Our life becomes a beautiful example to those observing.

We are going to examine a few of those spiritual weeds a little more closely. I'm trusting it will bring a life-changing revelation of deeper issues and help us understand why we need to uproot the invasive sins and clean up the garden of our soul.

Questions

What did working through the list show you about strongholds you are dealing with? Which did you identify that you had no idea existed? How do you feel since confessing and renouncing them?

As the days go by, what is God continuing to reveal about past issues? What life-weeds have taken you by surprise? Haven't heard anything from Him yet? Take time to sit quietly before Him and ask. He'll tell you.

What do you think of the analogy of burned-on food to unresolved issues? How does it help you to grasp the concept? Can you think of another analogy of your own?

What is your greatest take-away from this chapter?

You will find more about Satan and his names in Appendix B at the back of the book. Check it out!

Chapter Six
Through the Looking Glass

Proverbs 23:7 *"As she thinks in her heart, so is she."*

Jeremiah 17:10 *"I the Lord search the heart and examine the mind."*

The last chapter took us on quite an introspective journey. If you were like me, you would have had to sit on those pages for several days until the list had been fully dealt with. But now we move forward in greater freedom, looking more closely at a few more powerful issues of bondage.

When I was growing up, we had a giant magnifying glass my dad needed to read the tiny print in his massive concordance. He called it the looking glass. "Heather, find me the looking glass, please." I knew exactly what he meant and moved to do his bidding. Sometimes I moved too slowly and heard a slight Scottish accent surface as he spoke with more firmness, "Quickly, girl, I do not want to lose my place!" Then I knew it was time to move faster.

That looking glass allowed my dad to see the things he could not see with his natural eyes. Using this aid allowed him to see more clearly. The words were exposed in a greater way, and what he needed to read was revealed for him.

Let's look more deeply into a few of Satan's strategies, but first we are going to stop and ask the Holy Spirit to be our looking glass.

Sweet Holy Spirit, please lead us through this chapter, revealing things we need to grasp, and understand. Satan is trying to blind us to Your truth, but we are coming to You, trusting in Your power and goodness. Give eyes to see, hearts to understand, and minds to accept what You disclose. Hold us, and our families, in Your protective arms. We give You thanksgiving and praise. Amen.

Let's go.

Pride was Satan's sin, and when we see it in ourselves, it usually signifies his presence in some way. Pride is a door opener to disobedience and rebellion. God hates pride and warns us that if we allow it to reside within us, we are eventually going to take a spiritual tumble!

Proverbs 16:18 *"Pride goes before destruction, a haughty spirit before a fall."*

Unfortunately, although pride opens the door to evil behavior, wrong choices, and blatant disrespect, it also appears to be a characteristic admired in society. Pride is often seen as self-confidence and inner strength, which is attractive to many, drawing compliments and accolades. This can keep the dark spirit camouflaged and ignored, allowing it to remain unidentified. But pride is a dangerous resident to dwell in your soul, and it tries the patience of God.

In Daniel chapter four, we see King Nebuchadnezzar, the greatest of the Babylonian kings, warned by God to stop worshiping idols, stop worshiping himself, and start worshiping the living God. The king saw all the great miracles God had done for Daniel, Shadrach, Meshach, and Abednego and knew in his heart Daniel's God was worthy of all praise. Unfortunately pride in his accomplishments whisked him back into serious self-worship. God then fulfilled His warning and drove Nebuchadnezzar to live in the wilderness for seven years, out of his mind, eating grass like a cow and growing talons for nails. He had been reduced to an animal, until the day he finally raised his eyes to heaven and praised the Most High. Take a moment here to read the fourth chapter of Daniel and see the lesson this king learned about pride! It is quite an amazing story.

Stemming from pride is a **critical spirit.** At first glance, this can appear healthy and intelligent, an educated opinion or a wise approach. It is not. It is an insidious evil that also caused Satan's cast from heaven. Satan felt he could do a better job ruling the heavens than God, and he spread his criticism throughout the company of angels, swaying their thinking to align with his. One third of the angels in heaven fell for it and are now doomed to hell for eternity!

Satan loves it when we judge others and criticize them. It allows him to nurture the illegitimate thought that we are better than others. Our critical eye focuses on a poisoned comparison and distracts us from seeing our own faults. These negative thoughts almost always come out in our words and conversations, affecting relationships and our testimony. The more we feel justified to critique, the darker and darker our thoughts become. Our eyes soon turn from God and center on seeing negativity in everything. This spirit seeps into the marrow of our bones like a growing cancer, eventually spinning into deep-seated dissatisfaction.

Romans 2:1 delivers a warning. *"For in posing as a judge and passing sentence on another, you condemn yourself, because you who judge are habitually practicing the very same things!"*

It's that old adage: when you point a finger at someone, there are always three other fingers pointing back at you.

Matthew 7:1,2 AMPC says, *"Do not judge or condemn others so that you may not be judged and criticized and condemned yourselves. For as you judge, criticize and condemn others,* ***you*** *will be judged, criticized and condemned.* ***In accordance with the measure you deal out to others, it will be dealt out to you"*** (emphasis added).

A critical spirit is a slippery slope to God's refining fire, a good thing, but often painful through the process.

Lying is often referred to in the book of Proverbs. It talks about lying lips and deceitful tongues. It tells us a liar is a fool, lying endures only for a moment, God detests lying lips, and any gain from a lie lasts as long as a vapor. Proverbs 12:22 also warns, *"The Lord detests lying lips, but He delights in people who are trustworthy."*

Lying can be intentional or habitual. It can be used to mislead or destroy, protect or build up, be malicious or have no real purpose at all, but most certainly one lie leads to another and we know where that leads—a tangled web!

Proverbs 16:28 points specifically at women when it talks about **dissension**, which could also be called quarreling, a critical spirit, gossip, or scoffing. It says, *"A perverse woman stirs up dissension and a gossip separates close friends."*

I think we have all experienced that at some time—either as the propagator or the recipient.

If we insert the feminine version into 1 Timothy 6:3-5, we read, *"If any woman...does not agree to the sound instruction of our Lord Jesus Christ and to godly teaching, she is conceited and understands nothing. She has an unhealthy interest in controversies and quarrels about words that result in envy, strife, malicious talk, evil suspicions and constant friction between people."* (Putting it that way makes it more personal!)

Matthew 15:18,19 tell us, *"The **words** that come out of a woman's mouth come from the heart and these defile them. For out of the heart come evil thoughts, murder, adultery, sexual immorality, theft, false testimony, slander"* (feminine and emphasis added).

Wow. We cannot allow any ungodly thoughts to exist in us. They are far too dangerous if left alone. They will always be flung out as words we are sorry for but can't take back. Proverbs 18:21 (MSG) says, *"Words kill, words give life, they are either poison or fruit, you choose!"*

We will never regret things we say if we keep our words honoring to God. Perhaps before speaking harsh or critical words, we could quickly ask ourselves who will gain from what we're going to say. Satan or God? That may take just the time we need to clamp our mouth shut.

Jealousy, resentment, and bitterness can be big ones for us. They are powerful emotions often stemming from fear or insecurity. They are the emotions that caused Cain to kill his brother Abel, taunted Joseph's brothers to sell him as a slave, or had King Saul force David to run for his life. Notice where this spirit can lead. It never seems to end well.

Jealousy is considered a tormenting spirit because it affects everything we do and say. If never dealt with, it can last a lifetime, emerging as bitterness, envy, or hatred toward another. It usually involves holding grudges and unforgiveness to the point of destroying relationships. It can drive us to do nasty things, speak devastating words, damage another's reputation, and spread lies, all the while keeping *us* in a state of misery. Who wants that? Jealousy eats away at our health and propels us into a damaging downward spiral!

Resentment opens the door to the spirit of offense. When we allow this spirit to reside in our mind over one issue, it will spread quickly, and before long the list of people who offend us is shockingly long. The only person resentment hurts is the one holding on to it! It's as productive as cutting oneself and hoping the other person bleeds to death.

Bitterness settles deep in our soul like creeping rot. It doesn't stay in our soul but spreads to our demeanor and speech. We end up wearing it on our face and spewing it in our words. It appears in our social media comments and our conversations and finds a way to lick across the tail end of any compliment we manage to give. It colors our vision, twists our world, and feels like a raw wound that never stops bleeding. Nothing ages a person more than bitterness, and the lasting effects often include illness and disease. But perhaps the greatest tragedy of all is when people look at us, it's all they can see. They can no longer see Jesus!

Depression and anxiety abound in plague proportions today—both in Christians and non-Christians. More Christians are seeing counselors, psychologists, and psychiatrists than ever before. There are hundreds of books dealing with depression and anxiety on today's market, yet this particular issue still grips the masses.

Medications to treat these issues fill pharmacy shelves, wait in our pockets, and stuff our purses. Constant ads on television drive many to self-diagnose, and young children are prescribed powerful antidepressants to help them deal with a fear-mongered, bullying society. Still a cure is yet to be found.

The reasons for depression may be varied, but the manifestation is the same: darkness, despondency, hopelessness, and overwhelming fatigue. Anxiety develops into paralyzing fear, panic, and withdrawal from normal living. Neither of these states of mind are what God wants for His beloved daughters. They are what the enemy wants for us. Jesus came to give us abundant life. Depression and anxiety rob us of that. Satan cheers when God's girls are paralyzed by hopelessness and fear, but God offers us a way out.

There may be a time when the right medication is necessary, and there is no shame in intelligently using medicine. But we must not seek a savior in our pills. Our Creator is the One who heals.

Listen to God's encouragement.

Philippians 4:6 says *"Do not be anxious about anything, but in everything by prayer and petition, with thanksgiving, present your requests to God. And the peace of God, which transcends all understanding will guard your hearts and minds in Christ Jesus."*

Let's read that again, but this time as written in The Message. *"Don't fret or worry. Instead of worrying, pray. Let **petitions** and **praises** shape your worries into prayers, letting God know your concerns. Before you know it, a sense* *of God's wholeness, everything coming together for good, will come and settle you down. It's wonderful what happens when Christ displaces worry at the center of your life"* (emphasis added).

Can I get an Amen to that?

Satan loves when he is left to mess with our minds, even when there are legitimate reasons for despondency, such as illness or disease, trouble at work or trouble at home, too many kids or not enough, menstruation or menopause, loss or trauma, and fatigue or failure. Tying our emotions to our circumstances will keep us on a rollercoaster that gives the enemy an opening. He will piggy-back on our troubles every chance he gets and suck the life right out of us.

Then Satan is quick to fill us with guilt over our unwelcome emotions. He tells us good Christians don't get depressed, that fear is sin. He whispers that there is no hope for us— we're obviously a failure. He plants ideas that God loves us less and loves others more. And that He has turned His back on us. Soon voices softly suggest thoughts of death. The voices say it's the only way out, that suicide is a viable option and will remove the pain. Evil torments us with a belief that no one needs us anymore anyway and death will be a better solution for everyone.

Terrible, horrible, godless lies, every one!

So what is the answer? How can we dig out of the darkness?

Philippians 4:8 sheds hope on this overwhelming issue. *"Finally, sisters, whatever is true, whatever is right, whatever is pure, whatever is lovely, whatever is admirable—if anything* *is excellent or praiseworthy—**think...about...such...things!**"* (emphasis added).

If this is an issue that haunts you, may I suggest taking this verse to heart and making a long list of everything it suggests. Keep that list close to you, and when the shadows approach and you know the darkness is near, read through your list out loud as many times as needed and thank God for each and every item. This action takes power away from the enemy and fixes our eyes on Jesus, the author of our faith.

We cannot trust our emotions, girls. They are too volatile. They deceive us and lead us into unpleasant places. We need to take them to God, ask Him to lift them from us, and then turn our thoughts onto other things and move forward.

Look again at that list we are to think on—truth instead of lies, rightness instead of misconception, purity instead of evil, loveliness instead of darkness, things we admire instead of dread, things that are excellent instead of discouraging, and things worthy of our praise instead of criticism. There is One who fits all these suggestions—it's Jesus. Keeping our eyes on Him keeps our eyes off the enemy's ploys.

I also know a book where we can find these things to think upon—the Bible. They weave like a living vine from the beginning to the end. The Spirit of God is in that book, and His words can lift us from heaviness into the sunshine that warms and heals our aching soul.

Isaiah 61:1a,2b,3 *"The Spirit of the Lord is on me, because the Lord has anointed me to proclaim good news...to bind up the brokenhearted...to proclaim freedom...and release from darkness...to comfort all who mourn and provide for those who grieve...to bestow on them a crown of beauty instead of ashes, the oil of joy instead of mourning and a garment of praise instead of a spirit of despair."*

Our times of depression or anxiety matter to God because *we* matter to God. We are never alone in any situation, no matter what our emotions tell us. We have a mighty God walking with us, and when the path is just too hard to trod, He picks us up in His mighty arms and carries us.

Isaiah 46:4 *"Even to your old age and gray hairs I am He, I am He who will sustain you, I have made you and I will carry you; I will sustain you and I will rescue you."*

"If only" are two of the most destructive words in the English language (at least when they are put together). *If only* I had more time. *If only* I had more money. *If only* I had more freedom. *If only* my husband was more understanding. *If only* my kids were more obedient. *If only* I could lose weight. *If only* I looked like her. *If only* I had a better car. *If only* my hair was long or short or straight or curly. *If only* I had a bigger house or a housekeeper or a gardener or a nanny. *If only* I could find jeans to fit! *If only* my problem was solved, everything would be fine.

The problem is, when one of our issues is solved, there is always another waiting in the wings and nothing is ever *fine.*

When we dwell on the *if only,* we have taken our eyes off Jesus and placed them on our problems, our circumstances, our needs, and our wants. We give power to an evil that will keep us in perpetual torture! We are focusing on obstacles and defeat instead of trusting God and His power to provide and protect. God has promised us peace that passes understanding, but our *if only* mindset blocks that possibility. We sadly sink into negativity, missing out on ministry. I'm pretty sure we can all relate to this one, because we all do it at one time or another, and we have to stop. God can deliver us from this mind trap. We just need to ask.

We've already seen how God feels about **anger**. James 1:19 tells us, *"My dear sisters (and brothers), you should all be quick to listen, slow to speak and slow to become angry."*

Hmm. Slow to speak? James must not have had a lot of women in *his* life, heh, heh. None of those things come easily to most of us. Instead, we have a hard time listening, speak too quickly, and can become angry in an instant. James goes on to say that a woman's anger does not produce the righteous life God desires. The psalmist also warns us not to sin in our anger, as it stirs up strife. Apostle Paul reminds us in Ephesians 4 not to let the sun go down on our anger and to get rid of anger, rage, and bitterness, brawling slander, and every kind of malice. (Anger does a lot of damage when left unchecked.) Paul then says to replace it! Replace it with kindness, compassion, and forgiveness. Not an easy task. We need the help of the Holy Spirit!

When women see the term **sexual sins,** we immediately think that could not apply to us! That must only be for men. We tend to think we don't struggle with this sin and are mostly pure in this matter. But are we? Sexual sins do not just refer to the act of sex outside of marriage but also to things we allow into our thoughts and accept—perhaps through the watching of inappropriate TV shows or movies, reading romance novels, listening to seductive lyrics in music, tolerating sexual indiscretions in conversations and jokes, or dwelling on inappropriate thoughts. Temptations can creep into our life without our notice.

God told both Joseph and Paul what to do when these things arise. *Flee.* Turn off that TV and run from it. Close that book immediately and put it in the garbage. (Don't give it to your best friend or the library!) Stop dancing and singing along with that song, and don't laugh at the dirty joke. Flee.

Self-pity is a dark spirit evident to everyone but the one struggling with it. It pours from each conversation because it's as all consuming as an addiction. It often starts each sentence with the word *why.* Why can't I have a good marriage? Why can't I do anything right? Why does no one respect me? Why do I always get sick? Why does nothing ever work out for me? Why don't I ever have enough money? Why do bad things always happen to me? Why is everyone else's life better than mine?

This destructive attitude can begin as a learned behavior, then become habitual, infiltrating every thought. When that happens, we wear it like a garment!

Many years ago, I inherited a hundred-year-old, badly shedding, extremely heavy, black sheared-beaver coat from my grandmother. It takes up a lot of space in our front hall closet, and it's so heavy that when I wear it, I can barely move. At first it feels warm and comfortable, but in no time at all, I find it presses in, drags me down, drains my energy, and keeps me from enjoying an outing in the snow. When I get back inside and shed the thing, it's like losing twenty pounds.

That coat reminds me of self-pity. You may have inherited it or just allowed it to take up space in your attitude, but if you don't get rid of it, you will wear it like that heavy coat and it will make you, and everyone around you, miserable. It is impossible to indulge in self-pity and walk in the power of God. Joyce Meyer says, "You can be pitiful or powerful, but you cannot be both!"[8]

---

[8] Joyce Meyer, *Healing the Soul of a Woman.* FaithWords, 2018.

Questions

Which of these bondage traps strikes you as yours?

This is the best time to deal with whatever God is revealing to you. Find a quiet place, like your closet or in your car, and pray through this issue, asking God to cleanse, forgive, and heal you.

Thank God for His deliverance, and invite the Holy Spirit to fill the space in your life that is now cleaned out.

That was a cleansing chapter, but we aren't finished yet! Satan's list of ways to attack is long, and we are going to keep going until we deal with every single one of them. But as we pursue this journey, it gets easier to see truth, deal with the devil, and experience life-giving freedom. Totally worth it my friend, so keep going!

Chapter Seven
The Victory Dance

I know you will need to take a breath after that last chapter, but we aren't finished dealing with Satan's strategies. That old serpent finds places to hide in our thoughts where we seldom look. Satan wants us to think our thoughts are based on truth, but many times he has planted their seed. When we allow the seed to stay, they grow in strength, and we dwell on them. Then, he is in! When he has that little space in our minds, he will work hard to gain more ground until he has us where he wants us—angry, fearful, discouraged, or dissatisfied.

If you identify with any one of these, God has an encouragement for you.

• I wish I was pretty

I'm not going to lie to you. I am not enjoying the aging process that seems to be taking over. I have always appreciated makeup, but now it isn't quite doing the job. I've come to realize that product advertisements haven't been truthful! In case you haven't discovered this yet, let me fill you in. There is no moisturizer out there that can remove wrinkles. Nope. Not one. But as much as aging bugs me, the Bible tells me there is a different beauty I need to be more concerned with—my inner beauty—the place that reflects the beauty and glory of God in my life.

1 Samuel 16:7b says, *"The Lord does not look at the things people look at. People look at the outward appearance, but the Lord looks at the heart."*

What God sees in me is more important than the world seeing a few wrinkles and some age spots. But I know myself well, and the only way I'll be beautiful in my spirit is if God fills the space. His beauty gives me radiance. And that is what I want more than anything. I want to have the inner beauty of His presence so that when people look at me, they see Jesus!

• I'm worthless

This is such a paralyzing lie. Sometimes it grabs an early start in our life through careless words spoken over us, and sometimes it comes out of difficult relationships with children, husbands, mothers-in-law, parents, or siblings. Even though it may start with a word, it gradually grows into a belief that is straight from the devil. God does not think we are worthless; He tells us we are of great worth. After all, He does not create garbage! His creations are masterpieces. In fact, God thinks so much of us that He gave up His precious, beloved, only Son to die for us.

Look at John 3:16 and write your name in the blanks.

"For God so loved_____ that He gave His only precious Son, that if _____ should believe in Him, _____ shall not perish but have everlasting life!

If God gave His Son to be killed for you, you have to know you are of tremendous value to Him.

• I have rights!

"I have a right to be happy, to be loved, to have enough sleep, to have more *me* time, to do what I want to do and not always be looking after others." I've heard this often, and I'm sure you have too. Perhaps we have said a few of them ourselves. Actually sleep, rest, and happiness are all good things. We should appreciate those blessings when we have them. But everything we have are gifts from a loving God and not because we have a right to them.

To see this tantrum in a revealing way, find someone who has all the things you wish you had, and you'll still hear them complaining about something else. Having everything we want may sound good, but it does not bring the happiness we think it will. God wants us to be content. He even offers us peace that passes understanding, but it will not come in the way we think it will. It is only as we *give up* our rights and accept what God wants for us that we will have peace.

1 Peter 5:6 *"Humble yourselves, therefore, under God's mighty hand, that He may lift you up in due time. Cast all your anxiety on Him because He cares for you."*

• If I could just be married!

"If I could be married I would feel loved and valued." As much as society believes this, Christian women can have a tremendous peace and joy in finding all we need in Jesus. There can be great fulfillment in marriage, but there are also many women absolutely miserable in theirs! God has a plan for each of us, and He will use us whether we have a husband or not—sometimes in an even greater way if not. He wants to be the source of our peace and joy. When we give this issue over to God, He will work things out in His perfect timing and plan.

Psalm 37:4-6 *"Take delight in the Lord, and He will give you the desires of your heart. Commit your way to the Lord; trust in Him and He will do this: He will make your righteous reward shine like the dawn, your vindication like the noonday sun."*

• I can't go on like this!

Yes, sometimes life delivers difficult blows. It could be grief or betrayal, exhaustion or discouragement, temptation or confusion, anxiety or depression. These things can propel us into a pit that feels impossible to escape. Difficulties are part of living, and sadness seems unavoidable, but God wants us to know He is enough.

2 Corinthians 12:9 AMPC "*His grace is enough to see us through.*"

There is no greater comfort in this life than the comfort of the Holy Spirit sent in times of need. It softens the grief and dispels the sorrow. God has promised to give this if we come to Him with a heart of trust.

When things are bad, we can call on Jesus, call another Christian friend, reach out to a God-fearing pastor, or just search the Scriptures for truth when peace seems elusive. God is the God of hope. Romans 15:13 says, "*May the God of hope fill you with all joy and peace as you trust in Him, so that you may overflow with hope of the Holy Spirit.*"

• My kids are out of control!

"I don't know what to do!" Most of us moms have uttered those words at one time or another. We think we have done our best, but our kids seem to have a mind of their own.

They do. God has given every human being the gift of free will—the ability to choose whom they will serve—because the bottom line is, in this world we will either serve God or Satan.

What can we do to assure our kids will choose to serve God? Nothing. We can't have that assurance because of their free will. But we are given a tremendous opportunity while they are young to teach them the wonderful knowledge of the living God, to hear about His greatness, to see how He answers prayers, to know about His sacrifice made for us to have eternal life, and to experience His incredible love as we live out His truth before them. This is a blessing and a challenge given to parents who take this task seriously. May I suggest three things to help in this journey?

We can start by **praying** for them before they are born, after they are born, and every day after that. Prayer is the greatest tool a mother has, and we need to use it faithfully. God hears our prayers for our kids.

Second, we can **read** good, instructional Christian writing: authors such as Dr. James Dobson, Joyce Meyer, John Bevere, Mark Batterson, or Ted Tripp. There are as many good books on raising children to know God as there are methods, so look up what you need.

Third, you can **fast** and pray. I recommend Jentezen Franklin's book *Fasting* to learn more about this option. It is a powerful one, and the mother who is determined to bring God into the process will be delighted with the knowledge and encouragement his writing holds.

Generational sin

Generational sin is something different, yet still a powerful strategy to keep us defeated. It can be harder to identify, especially if you don't know your older relatives or have information on ancestors. But negative behavioral patterns repeating throughout generations can often be recognized, such as rage, anxiety, abuse, depression, and addiction. These issues tend to gain strength with every generation, but they also always seem easy to excuse. *Oh, she got that temper from her grandpa. Aunt Wilma suffered from depression too. Uncle Bill was an alcoholic, so I guess I inherited that from him. I grew up with chain smokers, so how could I be any different?*

There may be something you see in your children that you have seen in your parents or in-laws. Generational curses are usually deeply seated, and the power of prayer and fasting against them is needed. Prayer covering the next generations should be included in that process. Most issues can be bound up through prayer and the hold over the family broken. If the problem does not leave, add fasting to the process. Remember, spiritual victory and freedom tastes better than the most delicious meal, and rejoicing trumps any dessert!

I must insert a personal experience here. My elderly parents had sold their home and were moving to assisted living. My job as only daughter was to clean out and pack up the seventy years of collections and precious possessions. Through the process, I often brought home things I just didn't have the heart to throw out.

One day I pulled out a rolled-up paper that revealed a sketch of my grandparents. I shoved it back in the bag and took it home. It sat on our kitchen table for over three weeks as I continued my daily duties in getting my parents settled. One particular morning, I sat sipping my coffee and looked at the bag again. I shook out the rolled paper and opened it up. Out of the center slid an old, tightly rolled piece of parchment that had been hidden inside. I squinted at the tiny print in effort to understand what it was. The markings were strange—Egyptian-like. Further down the brittle, yellowed page I saw my grandfather's name. Looking more carefully, I realized it was a promotion certificate to a high level in a demonic "secret brotherhood" organization. There was a date on it. It was one hundred years ago to the day! Shock rippled through me. This was not a coincidence!

My grandfather had become a Christian in his later years, and as I was growing up, he told me about the night of his conversion. He also said at that time he instantly knew he could not remain in this private organization. He revealed that at a certain level they began occult practices. Even as a new Christian, he realized he could no longer be a part of this. When he asked to be removed from membership, it was granted, but he was required to take an oath to not reveal their secrets (and as far as I know he never did). He did warn us to steer clear and have nothing to do with them...ever. In this, my sweet, gentle grandpa was firm, unbending, and insistent.

Looking again at this paper, I realized the timing was God's. I felt God telling me this document came with generational issues. It may have been a portal for decades of demonic activity that had hounded our family for those hundred years. (I could think of many ways.) Laying on our kitchen table right then was a call to action, and the timing was obviously important. I was being appointed to take authority over this generational spirit and burn the paper before the next century began.

I yelled for my husband to come quickly, and Gord hurried down the stairs. "Where's the fire?" he puffed.

"Well," I held up the parchment, "it's going to be right here."

We read it through together and knew what God was asking us to do. We were to take authority over this document and what it represented, pray a prayer of repentance and deliverance, and then destroy it. And so we did—out loud, claiming the power of God Almighty over this curse, binding it in the name of Jesus Christ of Nazareth, sending the spirits back to the feet of Jesus of Nazareth, and claiming freedom for those still living under this influence in our family. We asked God to send strong angels to make sure this was accomplished. We asked for protection for our family and demanded no retaliation from the enemy. We then invited the Holy Spirit into this situation and asked Him to fill the places vacated by evil and seal our family by His power.

Then I picked out a new barbecue lighter and lit it. We turned our heads from the expected flames as I held it to the corner of this hundred-year-old piece of parchment. Nothing happened. I held it longer. And longer. And longer— because this paper would not burn!

Not to be discouraged, we went outside where Gord could use his flame-thrower, which he brought from the garage. We placed the dried-up old document in a pail and blasted it from three feet away. It still did not burn. Our deck was in more danger of cinderization than that old document! Gord held the ferocious flame on the ancient scrap of paper for twenty-five minutes until it was down to the size of a quarter, but no matter how long we continued, that last little piece would not burn up. How could this be? I finally took it out and ground it to dust. We prayed again, and went inside.

An important lesson was reinforced that day. Demonic spirits can inhabit *objects*. After doing serious research, we learned they can attach to things used by or made by anyone in witchcraft or plagued by demonic beings: articles, documents, paintings, houses (or a specific room in a house), vehicles, carvings, mirrors, and pretty much anything else. My grandfather had realized his exposure to the demonic in that private club, but he did not know that just leaving the well-known organization would not leave the dark world of evil behind. Spirits remain in what they feel is a rightful place until they are confronted and dealt with.

My husband Gord and I have established a mission in Haiti, a country where we experience the prevalence of Satan worship and the encompassing presence of the enemy. We pray God will keep evil out of our mission compound, asking each morning for strong angels at the gates and the Holy Spirit to fill our property with His presence. There are times we actually see the results of that prayer in protection and peace.

Canadian and American teams visit our mission throughout each year. At the end of their week, we bring in Haitian vendors to sell beautiful carvings, jewelry, paintings, and handcrafted items. But all things in our little market are faithfully prayed over, and our field director, Wouillio (a redeemed witch doctor), walks through to make sure these items are free from any demonic attachments that could be carried home.

Back in Canada when I walk through home décor stores, images stare at me from the shelves that smack of evil and idols: Buddhas, Hindu gods, crystals, horoscopes, and symbols of fertility and spiritism. I usually just walk past, but once in a while I'll pray protection over myself, and anyone that may be especially vulnerable that day. Once in a while, I say the name of Jesus out loud just to shake them up. Lol!

As long as we are talking about spirits attaching to objects, I'd like to interject another real-life experience that shows how evil uses this portal to attack our kids. For the purpose of anonymity, and good storytelling, I'll use a different name.

It was mid-morning and I was vacuuming the stairs when a vision of a toy popped into my mind's eye. It looked old and well loved, a harmless toy that could be found in anyone's toy box either today or in years past. I stopped vacuuming and waited. A single word came into my mind. The word was clear yet was one I did not understand. (I will not share that word here, and you will soon realize why.)

The vision of that toy and the single word that came with it stayed with me all that day, not like a pleasant tune sometimes does—more like a stone in my shoe or a sliver in my finger—uncomfortable and persistent. I went to my computer and Googled the word still ringing in my thoughts.

The word was described as one used by sorcerers and witch doctors when they want to cast a dark spell or curse. Now this vision took on clarity of meaning and was accompanied with urgency.

The toy was like something I remembered seeing in a friend's home, so I messaged her, "Lisa, I remember you showing me a toy once, one that had been handed down to your children from their grandparents, and...I just wondered what you had called it?"

"Oh, it came with a name when we got it. It has been in my in-laws' family for three generations." Lisa then told me the name, and it was the exact word given to me with the vision. I already knew there had been serious fear and sleep issues with one of the children in that home and some supernatural incidents with the grandparents. The purpose for this revelation was now obvious. But there was work to do.

I went into my prayer closet and talked to God. I asked permission to reveal all I had learned and asked for wisdom and guidance for this godly mother and strength for her to do what must come next. I was given peace for the task ahead.

Lisa is a solid Christian and has a growing knowledge of spiritual warfare and authority, so I called her and told her the whole story, including the meaning of the name and the necessity to get rid of the object immediately. Burning it and praying over it would be the most efficient and final way to rid the power held through this seemingly harmless toy.

She listened quietly, saying little, so I left it with her and continued to pray on my own. A month later, I got a message from her and a picture. The message said, "Everyone is out of the house today so I decided it was time to burn the toy. I prayed over it, bound whatever spirit was in it, covered my family with God's protection, and set it on fire, but something very unusual happened. The stuffed toy burned quickly, but the plastic eyes did not. In fact, they became brightly glowing embers, staring at me for over an hour until I couldn't take it anymore. I removed the eyes and ashes from the pail, took it out back and buried it. It's done." The picture she included showed two dots glowing in the pail, and I could almost hear evil screaming at its demise. I told her how proud I was of her and thanked God for providing a way.

104

That image of those burning eyes reminded me of a time in Haiti when we encountered one of our workers on the road. Evil spirits were tormenting him. His face was contorted, and his voice was deep and growly. He stopped to scream at us, and my husband said quietly, "Son, look at me." The voice then shouted, "No. I cannot look at you! You have fire in your eyes!"

The fire he saw was the Holy Spirit. Our eyes are the window to our souls, and through them the invisible world sees which source of power rules in us. The toy's eyes shone evil, and Gord's shone God. I want my eyes to shine like my husband's, glowing with the Holy Spirit.

Satan always does his best to defeat and control us, but arming ourselves with knowledge and truth will allow us to identify and rebuke his evil attempts. Let's look at another powerful way he tries to deceive.

Satan seeks to control us through counterfeiting

God is the Creator. Satan is the copycat. He cannot create life, but his greatest joy is to desecrate and destroy God's creation. He even assembled his own kingdom to reflect God's kingdom in structure and hierarchy. Just as God has a plan for our life, so does the devil. The difference is God's plans are for our good, to give us hope and a future (Jeremiah 29:11), but Satan's plans for us are failure, depression, fear, addiction, and everything else in opposition to God's plans (John 10:10).

Counterfeiting by nature means "so close to the real thing that it is difficult to detect." Satan's counterfeiting is just that. If we aren't watching for it, we can easily be deceived.

What's Satan's goal with his counterfeiting? He wants to draw us away from our faith with false beliefs and practices, giving him access into our life and choices. He knows if he can control our thoughts, he can control our life. So as Joyce Meyer says, "Think about what you are thinking about!"

Here are some ways Satan attempts to copy God's plan for us.

• Worship

God seeks our worship. Worshiping God is what we were created for! Worship is expressing feelings of adoration. We worship anything we revere, give honor to, or give top priority to. We worship what is first and foremost in our thoughts. We are worshiping the things we give most of our attention and favor to. So we need to ask ourselves, with our busy schedules and draining responsibilities, how often is most of our attention and favor on God?

In Haiti, the national religion is voodoo, which is Satan worship. There is no need to disguise it, as it is an accepted form of worship. Satan's name is feared in most homes, and his power is taught to the youngest. There are many temples and peristils (open, pole-barn style temples) dedicated to his worship and servitude.

In North America, it is not usually that open and obvious. Although there is a growing culture of Satanism, we aren't always aware of it. We tend to worship less dangerous things like, food, clothes, possessions, status, celebrities, technology, wealth, talent, and security. *We* don't see it as worship, but as we discussed, anything we put more time, thought, and effort into than we do our relationship with God, is exactly that. Satan may not be as visual in North America, but he is just as busy keeping us from the worship God deserves.

• Family

A tight, loving, God-fearing family is a threat to Satan. He does his best to rip it apart. He will use things like private clubs, sports, technology, social media, broken relationships, busyness, and even church groups and programs taking the place and attention our family may need. If he can undermine family time, the devil is happy. When the kids find themselves regularly eating from the microwave instead of at the dinner table, he sees it as a victory.

• God's voice

How wonderful it is when we believe we have heard from God. He does speak to us, in many different ways, but I'm sure Satan gets a big kick out of speaking into our thoughts and watching us get excited about what we believe God has told us. Then when it doesn't happen the way we believe God said, we are disappointed, disillusioned, perhaps even confused or angry. But Jesus warned us to test the spirits, make sure what we hear aligns with God's Word and what we know of His character, perhaps even requesting confirmation before being too dogmatic.

• False teaching

Peter, Jude, Paul, and others warned of false teachers who bring pseudo doctrines. If what you are learning does not line up with Scripture, it needs to be regarded skeptically. If we take everything we read or hear as from God, we could quickly find ourselves believing a lie and frustrated in our faith. That is exactly how cults get started: new age philosophy, prosperity gospel, scientology, Jehovah's Witnesses, Mormonism, and cults like Davidians, Jonestown, Moonies, Hare Krishna. There are also false doctrines like the one perpetrating there is no hell and all people are going to heaven. Anything that does not teach Jesus as the Son of God and Messiah, and Scripture as absolute truth, is a counterfeit faith.

• Righteousness

Satan is very skilled at counterfeiting God's righteousness in us by installing a spirit of self-righteousness. The line between the two may seem vague and blurry, but it is acutely defined in God's eyes.

Self-righteousness is when we see ourselves as righteous apart from the righteousness of God given to us when we are redeemed. It inhabits the idea that we can do all things through our own strength. "You can be anything you want to be. You can do anything you want to do. You are all you need to be successful. You are like God."

In Romans 10:2,3 the author describes the Israelites: "*For I can testify about them that they are zealous for God, but their zeal is not based on knowledge. Since they did not know the righteousness of God and sought to establish their own, they did not submit to God's righteousness.*" Deceived...deluded... counterfeited.

It's imperative we arm ourselves against this deception. We need to know what the Bible teaches therefore we need to study our Bibles! Scripture reveals truth. It holds the key to wisdom and discernment, preparing and equipping us for battle. If we don't know what God says, how will we know when He is the one speaking to us?

Satan's end game is to render us completely useless in whatever way he can, so we live incapacitated in our faith. He wants us ineffective in kingdom building and constantly in a state of hopelessness and defeat. We've talked about his goal as basically to paralyze us emotionally and spiritually. We cannot allow him that freedom. We know this is not what God wants or has planned for His children.

Scripture tells us Jesus came to give us a spirit of power, of love, and of a sound mind! (2 Timothy 1:7) Jesus also said, *"The thief comes to steal, kill and destroy, but I came to give you life and life more abundantly!"* (John 10:10).

God has given us all the tools we need to have victory over Satan and to live in spiritual, emotional, and physical freedom.

So what are they? Six things: confess, repent, renounce, compare, commit and claim! That's a mouthful so let's break these down, one by one.

1. **Confess** to God areas you recognize Satan has gained ground.

2. **Repent** and ask forgiveness for these particular issues that have been revealed to you.

3. **Renounce** this sin, putting it from you, and determine to make a 180-degree change in your life in regards to these areas.

4. **Compare** everything you are hearing and thinking to Scripture. God's Word reveals truth. It teaches you, prepares you, and equips you to do battle.

Hebrews 4:12 *"For the word of God is alive and active. Sharper than any double-edged sword, it penetrates even to dividing soul and spirit, joints and marrow; it judges the thoughts and attitudes of the heart."*

5. **Commit** to being vigilant in identifying demonic attacks. Commit to embarking on a new spiritual journey and accountability to God. Commit to living a life as free from sin as possible. **Commit** to taking a stand and standing your ground against the enemy, and commit to growing in your faith through study and memorization.

Proverbs 10:25, *"When the storm has swept by, the wicked are gone, but the righteous stand firm forever."*

6. **Claim** the blood of Jesus and the authority given over yourself and your family. The definition of authority is "delegated power." Through Jesus' death and the blood He shed on the cross, *all power* over Satan gained through Adam's sin was won back. At His ascension, Jesus then delegated it to His followers—all those who have put their faith and trust in Him. (That's us!)

The power of the blood of Jesus runs deep. It is a symbol of purification and cleansing, the evidence of what took place on the cross. It was the shedding of His blood on Calvary that perfectly expressed His love for us. At the same time it provided forgiveness for our sin, healing of our diseases, fellowship with God, and victory over the vile works of the devil.

Revelation 12:10b-11a *"For the accuser of our brothers, who accuses them before our God day and night, has been hurled down. They triumphed over him by the blood of the Lamb."*

1 Peter 1:18,19 *"For you know that it was not with perishable things such as silver or gold that you were redeemed from the empty way of life handed down to you from your forefathers, but with the precious blood of Christ, a lamb without blemish or defect."*

Wow. The blood of Jesus holds tremendous power for the believer. We see in Exodus where the children of Israel required a blood sacrifice for protection. When they put blood on their doorposts, the angel of death God was sending would pass over them, unable to touch their children!

When we plead the blood of Jesus over our children, there is an unleashing of holy power that moves in miraculous ways!

Let's be intentional in removing all things not of God from our life and be ready to submit to God's cleansing each time sin rears its ugly head. Confession is not a one-time-fixes-all process. When we make it a part of the beginning of each day, it can become second nature. And as we gain ground against the enemy, he will retreat.

When we invite God (the light) into the darkness (our sin), the darkness loses power. John 1:5 (MSG) says *"The Life-Light blazed out of the darkness; the darkness couldn't put it out."*

Before long that issue will become weaker, show up less, and we will be doing a victory dance of worship and praise to our mighty God!

Take this to heart, dear friend, there is nothing, *nothing*, God cannot deliver us from!

Questions

What did you learn about the enemy's strategies that you did not know before? How will this knowledge change your life?

How do you relate to the "if only" struggle? List the ones you say the most. Ask God to prompt you to ask forgiveness whenever you say those again.

What thoughts create your greatest battles? Is something drawing your worship other than God? Make a list. What is your new game plan to deal with these?

Are you able to identify what could be a generational curse in your family? If so, ask God how He would have you deal with that.

Write out the six things to do to find freedom from Satan's strongholds.

Look again at all the issues dealt with in chapters five, six and seven. Have you been able to identify all the ones affecting your life? Has anything else popped into your mind that you should release to God? If so, you may want to do that now.

Why not put on your favorite worship music and do a victory dance of spiritual freedom around the house? Well, go ahead. I do it all the time. I think it makes God smile.

Chapter Eight
Dressed for Success!

"Mommy?" The sun had barely peeked over the horizon when my three-year-old son called me from the bedroom doorway. "Mommy, I'm hungry. Can I have breakfast?" Opening one eye I saw he had dressed himself but had chosen mismatched socks.

"Pete," I mumbled, "your socks don't match. One has a red stripe and the other has a green stripe. We'll get breakfast as soon as you change them." I hoped it would take a while and give me a few more moments of desperately needed shut-eye.

He ran to his bedroom but reappeared seconds later, still sporting the unmatched socks. Giant tears now threatened to spill down his pudgy cheeks.

"Son," I yawned, "I told you to change your socks."

"I did," he wailed, "but there was only another pair just like them!"

Barely stifling a giggle, I got up to give him a little hug and help him put together the right pair. I knew as the day progressed, negative comments over the socks would pick up speed, especially from his sisters, upsetting him even more. Pete would then be dealing with challenges all day long—all because his socks didn't match.

My precious boy's day was off to a bad start because he didn't have the right outfit. As an experienced mom, I knew getting dressed properly would help everything go better, not just for him, but for us all.

God doesn't care if our socks match, but He *has* given us a perfectly designed outfit to start our day on the right foot. This outfit has a custom fit, and each piece complements the other. It's a spiritual suit of armor, with every piece designed to help us successfully maneuver our day. Each item we put on has a purpose either to protect from the enemy or to give us courage to stand against him. When we are dressed in this armor, we can walk in freedom and power. The complexion of our day is different, and the challenges before us seem less daunting.

In Ephesians 6:10-18, we see all the pieces of armor set out. It looks heavy, and perhaps a little cumbersome, but God has been precise, providing complete protection for every part of our body. Although most of the pieces are to defend ourselves, there are one or two with a different purpose. Let's look at them as laid out for us in Scripture.

*"Finally, be strong in the Lord and in His mighty power. Put on the full armor of God, so that you will be able to stand firm against the schemes of the devil. For our struggle is not against flesh and blood, but against the rulers, against the authorities, against the powers of this dark world and against the spiritual forces of evil in the heavenly realms. Therefore put on the full armor of God, so that when the day of evil comes, you may be able to stand your ground, and after you have done everything, to stand. Stand firm then, with the **belt of truth** buckled around your waist, with the **breastplate of righteousness** in place, and with your **feet fitted** with the readiness that comes from the gospel of peace. In addition to all this, take up the **shield of faith**, with which you can extinguish all the flaming arrows of the evil one. Take the **helmet of salvation** and the **sword of the Spirit**, which is the word of God. And **pray** in the Spirit on all occasions with all kinds of prayers and requests. With this in mind, be alert and*

always keep on praying for all the Lord's people" (Ephesians 6:10-18, emphasis added).

Wow! I know that seems like a lot to remember and perhaps somewhat intimidating, but let's remember whom we serve. We are women of the living God! He not only promises to provide the wardrobe, He's also right there with the measuring tape and pins to make them fit! Then He forms us, His rank and file, into solid battle formations. Remember, when God call us, He equips us, or as a friend of mine says, "God doesn't call the qualified, He qualifies the called!"

We do nothing in our own power, but go forward in the power of Almighty God.

Check out our armor, and watch each piece nudge you in answering the call to action.

The helmet of salvation

When I look at the helmet of salvation, I always think of two things.

First I think of the many times my husband, kids, and grandchildren have been saved from terrible sports injuries by wearing a helmet. Our family is accident-prone but also jam-packed with dedicated athletes. Not a good combination! There have been many stitches, sprains, and broken bones, but the brains, thank goodness, have remained intact! (Although there have been times this could be questioned.)

The second thing I think of is the "slough of despond" from John Bunyan's *Pilgrim's Progress* (best book ever) or the "bog of despair" from *Princess Bride*. Both references need no description. I coil in horror, as images of swamps filled with mud and nasty creatures come to mind. But what has that to do with the helmet of salvation?

We now know that our mind is the prime target for Satan, and our thoughts are the place where he wins most battles. Despondency, depression, despair, worry, anxiety, hopelessness, and fear can settle into our thoughts. The longer they remain, the deeper they dig in. When the weeks, months, and years go by without their extraction, we think of them as just "who we are" and not dangerous enemy fire. The deeply entrenched thoughts eventually paralyze us. Our spiritual vision is blurred. We become so defeated, freedom seems just too great a struggle.

As you can see, this piece of equipment, the helmet, is incredibly important. It not only saves us from the power of Satan's attacks, the helmet focuses our mind on our salvation. It helps keep our eye on the prize! Salvation is only from Jesus Christ and comes with the spirit of power, of love and of sound mind. That knowledge can keep us moving into battle and confronting the enemy, because we know what we have been saved for.

It also allows us to know what we have been saved *from*. When we accept Jesus Christ into our life, we become a child of God, no longer subject to Satan. The grave has no power over us for we have eternal life. Hell is not in our future!

Through salvation, our thought patterns change to align with God's and our beliefs are transformed by the renewing of our minds. Salvation also gives us the gift of the Holy Spirit, an invaluable ally in fighting the formidable opponent.

The helmet of salvation covers and protects us as we live our daily lives allowing God to work through us to live victoriously and unhindered by the strategies of the enemy.

So before heading into battle, I ask you, "Do you have your helmet of salvation?"

The belt of truth

God is in every way the opposite of Satan. Satan is a liar and the father of lies, a master deceiver. God is truth, absolute truth, and our source of victory in the battle. It's with God's belt of truth that we fight Satan most effectively.

In ancient days of war, the soldier pulled his flowing garment from the back, forward through his legs, and tucked it into the wide, firmly buckled belt at the front. The belt held everything together and allowed him to fight unencumbered. It is in binding up all forms of deceit and dishonesty in our lives that we are able to go forward in our faith unhindered. We need to be open and honest in all our dealings with people and with God! The truth in scripture must live out in our lives whether it is popular or not.

Today, as women warriors, we fight the enemy with God's truth firmly guarding our minds, our thoughts, and our understanding, knowing truth is what holds our words and actions together. If we don't, there's always too much garbage flapping about our brains, interfering, deceiving, and distracting from the job at hand. Not accepting God's words as truth could place us in jeopardy, for it can only be truth that brings us to a place of victory.

Satan used lies and half-truths to deceive Eve, and he will use them on us. He hid the reality of consequences while propagating the illusion of "God is holding back and you deserve better." It's through a growing knowledge of the Word of God and His promises that we are equipped to identify and stand against this deception.

Second Timothy 3:7 delivers a strong warning to women. It talks about ungodly people who worm their way into our homes in an effort to gain control over those of us who are loaded down with spiritual burdens and swayed by evil desires—women who are always learning but never able to come to a knowledge of the truth.

Yes, that is always a possibility if we aren't allowing the things we are learning in Scripture to change us—if we're not willing to give up our wants and desires and accept what God wants for us. Only a strong belief in the truth and power of our holy God will keep us from crumpling under fire. Standing firm in the truth helps everything else fall into place.

The shield of faith

In the days of Roman occupation when Paul wrote Ephesians, the warrior's shield was used as protection from fiery arrows and wielded swords. Not only could a soldier hold it up to keep the darts from penetrating, but there was a beveled edge around that piece of armor that allowed shields to click together to form a gigantic wall, allowing soldiers to plow through everything the enemy had set up to stop them, marching forward in unity, shoulder to shoulder.

There is power in unity, and God is clear how important this is. We are called to click together in faith. When one of God's children is feeling attacked and weak, believers come alongside them, pray for them, and walk through the hard times with them as a unified force.

But the shield was heavy, and a soldier had to be physically fit to keep it in place. We also need to be fit, spiritually fit, to keep our faith strong and always ready to move into battle, covered by the shield of faith. That requires a spiritual workout each day in the form of meeting with God.

Satan's arsenal never seems to run out. He is firing those darts as fast as our shield deflects them. His goal is to injure, cripple, paralyze, defeat, and destroy. He is quite creative in the darts he chooses. His specialty for women seems most often to be fear:

- fear of failure
- fear of ridicule
- fear of abandonment
- fear of illness
- fear of loss
- fear of rejection
- fear of being hurt
- fear of uncertainty
- fear of change
- fear of loneliness
- fear of loss of freedom
- fear of worthlessness
- fear of aging
- fear of spiritual defeat

Fear is a biggie, and you may have a completely different one to add to this list.

We want to do things well—to make a difference and to matter. Satan's darts can take us down in a matter of minutes if we don't use the armor God gives us. Our faith in Jesus is the shield we need to snuff out the fear.

The "faith" part of this piece of armor is never faith in ourselves, nor faith in some mantra or creed. That would be disastrous. It is faith in God, in Jesus, and in the work of the Holy Spirit. We learn in Hebrews 11:6 that "*without faith it is impossible to please God.*" Jesus told His disciples that if we even have faith the size of a tiny mustard seed, we can move mountains! (Matthew 17:20).

What exactly is faith? Hebrews 11:1 tells us faith is "*being confident in what we hope for and certain of what we do not see.*" Faith is not saying, "I think," it's saying "I know!"

Faith is also depending on God in every situation, every challenge, every disaster, every disappointment, and everything going right. It is knowing God is in control and believing His will is best, no matter what that looks like. Faith is not always easy, nor is it for the faint of heart. It calls on all we have in us to bend our knee and trust in the Omniscient One.

But faith is more than just belief; it's also a call to action. It's not just what snuffs out the flaming end of the arrow and stops it from piercing our heart, the shield of faith is essential to advancing in battle and taking ground back from the enemy. Faith is a crucial part of our warrior wardrobe!

James 2:20,26 "*Do you want evidence that faith without deeds is useless? As the body without the spirit is dead, so faith without deeds is dead.*"

True faith will be more than a word to us—it will be the driving force behind every decision, it will be the act of obedience to God, and it will carry us through the dark nights of our life to rejoicing in the morning. Faith, even in the smallest of things, provides powerful protection in our biggest battles against the enemy.

The breastplate of righteousness

Righteousness is a curious word. The dictionary describes it as uprightness, adhering to moral principles, good, just, and sound. The Scriptures refer to it as holiness. Ephesians 4:24 in The Message talks about righteousness. *"Take on an entirely new way of life...a God-fashioned life, a life renewed from the inside and working itself into your conduct as God accurately reproduces His character in you."*

Righteousness is a gift won through Jesus' death, burial, and resurrection. It is *His* righteousness that we wear, allowing Him to reshape our character to reflect His.

During battle, the breastplate covered the soldier's vital organs. This is critical! When Satan fires his darts of accusation at us, Christ's righteousness covers us, keeping them from penetrating our heart and taking us down. Proverbs 4:23 tells us to *"guard [our] heart above all else, for it is the source of life."*

Our physical heart supplies the blood source to the rest of the body for health and vitality. Our spiritual heart supplies the source of truth, wisdom, and discernment that energizes us in our faith walk. It sustains us when we need sustaining and revives us when we need reviving. The spiritual heart is the center of the soul. Our soul is our personality, nature, will, emotion, and conscience. That's a lot of ground for the enemy to attack, and protecting the heart is essential as the enemy attempts to strike with ferocity. Unrighteousness is the only invitation Satan needs to open fire and strike a powerful blow. If we don't put on the breastplate of righteousness, he will take advantage, and we will find ourselves in serious trouble with issues of sin.

Put simply, righteousness is living a life pleasing and obedient to God, through the power of the Holy Spirit, who is given to us when we confess our sin and ask Jesus into our life. At that very moment, this piece of armor is instantly installed, breaking the back of Satan's strategy to destroy us. With God's righteousness firmly in place, we go on to fight another day as victors.

The sword of the Spirit

Hebrews 4:12 *"For the word of God is living and active and sharper than any two-edged sword, and piercing as far as the division of soul and spirit, of both joints and marrow, and able to judge the thoughts and intentions of the heart."*

The sword of the Spirit is not only for our protection; it is also an offensive weapon, meant for moving forward to mount an attack. It is the Holy Word of God—Scripture.

The sword of the Spirit is sharp and has life and power. The sword of the Spirit was what Jesus used against Satan in the great temptation of Christ. Every time Satan proposed a misbehavior, Jesus answered with *"It is written...,"* then quoted Scripture from the Old Testament and shut the devil down.

This piece of armor tells us that God wants us to be more than protected in the battle against the enemy and his sordid kingdom. He wants us aggressively taking Satan on when the challenges arise.

Matthew 16 talks about the keys we have been given to the kingdom of heaven and how they allow us to bind things on earth that will then be bound in heaven. There are many biblical scholars who believe this to mean God's children are able to stand before the gates of hell and take back what Satan has stolen, like our relationships, our health, our faith in God, and our family. **We can be victorious women when we wield the sword of the Spirit.**

One of my favorite passages is 2 Corinthians 10:3-5. *"For although we live in the world, we do not wage war as the world does. The weapons we fight with [God's Word] are not weapons of this world. On the contrary, they have divine power to demolish strongholds. We demolish arguments and every pretention that sets itself up against the knowledge of God, and we take captive every thought, making it obedient to Christ."*

A reminder of caution here; we use this weapon when all other pieces of armor are in place. This is the last piece we are told to put on, and until we are covered with salvation (helmet) and filled with the Spirit of God, we are not properly armed against this very powerful enemy. However, when we put all the pieces on in faith, we'll be prepared to take our stand, stand our ground, engage in battle, and win.

The shoes of peace

Every woman knows that an outfit is never finished until the perfect pair of shoes has been added. God knows that and has amazingly included a pair, perfect for the mission and completing our equipment with style!

I have to admit, I was so busy raising my passel of kids that what I put on my feet most days took last place. I took shoes for granted and sometimes found myself leaving the house in slippers! But there was a day this changed.

My oldest daughter, was about to be married, the first of my children to wed. I just knew I was going to fall apart, probably sobbing loudly through the entire ceremony, spoiling the whole thing and making a spectacle of myself. I shared these fears with a friend, and she gave me the most unusual advice. "When you buy shoes to go with your outfit," she said, "make sure they are at least one size too small."

"Huh?" was my brilliant response.

"Well, during the service, your feet will ache so much you won't be able to think of anything else and won't have to deal with the overwhelming emotions. You'll be more concerned about getting out of those shoes and not so much with losing your little girl."

Surprisingly, she was right. I found a sweet pair of iridescent pink heels to match my pink suit and made sure they were extremely snug. On the sweltering hot wedding day, as I watched my beautiful daughter walk down the aisle, I choked up for an instant but was so busy shifting my weight from one swelling foot to the other, my emotions stayed in check. A few tears managed to sneak silently out but at least remained unnoticed. The rest of the ceremony went well. I went home barefoot and blistered but relieved I hadn't ruined the event.

We all know that shoes can be our best friend or our worst enemy. They can bless or curse, protect or injure, bring us peace and joy, or rob us of both. But the shoes God gives us to complement our outfit are a perfect fit, able to endure the wear and tear, cushion us with comfort, and do no harm. He calls them the shoes of peace.

We don't often give a lot of importance to this piece of armor, but when you think of it in spiritual terms, we know that one of Satan's most powerful tools is to rob us of peace—peace of mind, peace in our family, peace in relationships, and peace with God. The enemy continually attempts to disrupt, destroy, confuse, and fill us with anxiety and discouragement. He gains great ground when he steals our peace. I believe the peace of God in our lives must be his worst nightmare, because it is something he cannot give, and this is what he attacks most often!

Jesus knows this and promised in John 14:27, *"Peace I leave with you; My peace I give you. I do not give to you as the world gives. Do not let your hearts be troubled and do not be afraid."*

Satan knows that when we are at peace with God, at peace with others, and at peace with ourselves, his power over us is greatly diminished.

War and Peace! It may be a successful name for a book, but the words just don't seem to go together. Yet God has supplied us with the ability to pursue both at the same time. These amazing shoes of peace walk us into the blazing battle but can keep us amazingly calm. We are called to look for peace in every situation, seek peaceful solutions, speak peaceful words, *pray* for peace, thank God for His peace, and go forward with peace in our hearts and an attitude of peace toward others.

It is easy to spot a woman wearing God's shoes of peace. You've seen her. She stands out because her life is a living example of how God uses us to bring Him glory and honor in what we say, the way we react, and how we behave.

A woman at peace is a beautiful thing. It draws others to her. Jesus becomes more visible in her life, and the gospel is preached not just in words, but in actions!

I may often make mistakes,
but I'll always be forgiven.
For I'm a child of the King
and now I'm bound for heaven.

I was planned. I've a purpose.
God's gifts will never cease.
I know you may not see it,
but I'm my Father's masterpiece!

Old Satan's rants and roaring
don't bother me a bit,
'cause I'm on my way to Glory,
and he's heading for the pit.

I've a helmet of salvation
I'm wearing like a crown.
My shield of faith and sword of truth
will bring the devil down!

I've got the Spirit of God's power
of love and discipline,
and the serpent will be sorry
when he coaxes me to sin.

For the Master's walking with me,
And calms me with His peace.
His Spirit will not leave me,
Nor will His mercies cease.

Questions

What does wearing the "helmet of salvation" mean to you in your everyday life?

Is always speaking the truth an issue for you? How has Satan used lies to complicate your life? How does seeing that truth holds everything together change things for you going forward?

Which one of Satan's fiery darts listed causes you the most trouble? How does recognizing it as an attack help you deal with it?

What places in your heart need protecting? Read Zechariah 3:1-10 and Philippians 3:8-9 to learn more about the righteousness of God given to you.

Have you ever been robbed of peace by a pair of shoes? Were your thoughts on goodness and righteousness right then, or were you cranky and belligerent? Why do you think God chose shoes to identify with walking every day in His peace?

Chapter Nine
Special Delivery

The church was packed. The woven palm fronds allowed a little breeze to sweep over the congregation, but it also allowed small squares of hot sun to stream across our shoulders. Each wooden bench bulged with bodies dressed in their very best, swaying side to side in unison, keeping time to the heart-felt worship music led with an accordion, an old keyboard, and a trumpet. Once again I thanked God for the opportunity to worship with the church at our mission in Haiti. Here God always feels close enough to hug.

As communion elements were passed, the singing moved into "What can wash away my sin? Nothing but the blood of Jeeesuuus."

Instantly a young man, recently baptized, jumped to his feet. He began shaking his fist in the air and yelling foul words and obscenities to no one in particular. I strained to look at his face. His normally sweet features were now distorted and twisted. The voice coming from him was deep and angry, not his own. It was obvious to us all he was being demonized.

As the shouting continued, I wondered why the pastor or elders did not stop the service to pray. They just kept singing and passing the wine and crackers while my young friend squeezed passed others sitting on the bench to stand in the aisle and continue his tirade. Eventually two elders came and stood just in front of him but didn't touch him.

The congregation kept on singing about the blood of Jesus! No one even looked at him as they sang on, waving their hands in praise. It amazed me.

Then something changed. The lad lurched backwards, as if an invisible fist punched him in the chest. The elders took one step toward him. Again and again he was pushed backwards by that invisible force until he was right out of the church structure. Each time the elders had nonchalantly moved with him, and now they circled the angry fellow and began to pray.

I watched, intrigued and curious. My husband and I had dealt with evil spirits on a different level before, but this was my first time watching how Christians raised in a culture steeped in voodoo dealt with the demonic.

As the young man was prayed over, I watched a miracle take place. His face returned to normal, his yelling ceased, and his body slumped with fatigue. The elders went back to the service, and my young friend went to sit under a huge mango tree just inside our gates, his head resting in his trembling hands. It was over for now, but we would deal with this again over the next few days until this young believer found complete freedom and deliverance from some powerful demons.

When I had the chance, I asked the pastor why they did not stop the service to pray over him. He simply said, "Ahh...the devil always wants to disrupt us when we sing about the blood of Jesus," he shrugged, "so we don't let him."

I was touched by such simple, yet deep wisdom. There was no fear, no drama, just people covered in Jesus' shed blood moving forward in faith and obedience. As I learned more about their uncomplicated approach to spiritual warfare, I became encouraged and excited to step up to the calling of helping others find freedom.

Back in Canada, I felt the hand of God (and my daughter Becki's) pushing me to write about this and many other incidents experienced on the frontline of spiritual warfare. To be honest, I was hesitant. I'd learned from my previously written books of redemption stories out of Haiti that demonic oppression was not widely accepted in North America. Many people don't want to hear that Satan has any power or influence over us. It either scared them, or they thought I made it up. But as I saw women struggling with things I knew to be attacks by the enemy, it seemed important to share what I was learning. I wanted them to find freedom from their sorrows, fears, and discouragements. I had seen God's victory over Satan, and desperately wanted it for God's women. Yet I said little.

Over the following year, Becki kept pushing and the Spirit kept tapping, so I continued my studies on this topic—but didn't start to write.

When I felt God's pressing in about this project I knew it was disobedient to not respond, but before beginning I must make sure I was protected and clean before the Lord. There could be nothing outside of God's Spirit leading me, or I could quickly be listening to the wrong voice and wander from the truth. The thought shook me. It was time to get to work, but I first needed to sit before Almighty God.

When my husband left for a one-week trip, it seemed to be that time I needed. So I pulled ten of what I felt were my most powerful books on spiritual warfare from my library and began reading them again, underlining, highlighting, and making copious notes. By the second day I was reading the third book, *Bondage Breaker* by Neil Anderson. and found myself under conviction as I began praying through the list of strongholds we allow in our life—things that

Satan could use to gain influence over me. (We saw many of them on pages 52-53.)

At first I read quickly, but I soon found myself hovering over a few. God was revealing many things that I'd allowed in without realizing it—resentments, bitterness, a critical spirit, and insecurities disguised as appropriate, normal, righteous, and virtuous! I was appalled.

I started again at the beginning of the list, named each one out loud asking God's forgiveness, and invited the Holy Spirit to fill the space vacated by God's cleansing (exactly like we did in chapter five). But the vast number of things overwhelmed me. I soon found myself on my knees with my forehead pressed to the floor, as though God's powerful hand had pushed me there. Over the next few hours, there was a great deal of sorrow and repentance, then joy of forgiveness and purifying. I got up feeling like a different person—lighter and filled with a peace beyond comprehension.

The next morning I felt all had been dealt with and began my morning in prayer ready to hear from the Lord. What I heard was shocking. Issues that went back years into my past started to pop into my memory. I confessed each as it was revealed, but all that day they kept coming. How on earth could I have suppressed so many things?

The next day was the same, and the day after that! Faces, words, thoughts, actions, experiences, hurts, trauma, reactions, resentments, and unkindness—everything still needing to be dealt with. Part of me wanted to shout, "Lord, stop! I can't deal with any more!" But the other part desperately wanted to finish this. So, I kept on.

On day six I sat down with my pen and paper and asked, "Okay God, what do You have to reveal to me today that I need to confess?"

There was just sweet, blessed quiet! It appeared *that* journey was over—for now. There would be more in my future, I realized, but right then I was clean before God, delivered of things hindering the task at hand. I was now ready to hear what God wanted me to learn.

I finished the rest of the books, reading all day and into the night, but on day seven, God called me to do something I would never have dreamed of doing, and like Moses I argued with God.

Over the past few days, He had shown me a generational issue that had affected our family life. I loved my dad and knew he loved me, but growing up, my brother and I experienced some real rage issues from our father. We never really knew when he would blow, but when he did it wasn't pretty.

I must be clear here. Dad loved Jesus. He had a brilliant mind and loved studying Scripture. He had been an elder in our church, a spiritual leader in our city, a vocal advocate for keeping the Lord's Prayer in schools, an itinerant preacher, and a respected and well-known chiropractor who shared his faith at every chance with anyone who would listen. Dad ran a yearly Spiritual Life Conference in the city and used his holidays to visit mission fields and treat missionaries. He visited the sick, he worked in prison ministry, and he prayed over anyone who needed prayer. My dad was a godly man.

But a memory I had suppressed came back. A couple of times during one of Dad's rages, I had seen his face change. That memory reminded me of the young Haitian man's face when being demonized. Both their faces had been distorted during the rant. Then I thought of conversations with Dad over the years about how angry *his* father had been and apparently often mean. It was like an "aha" moment for me. One I did not relish. It seemed there could be a generational curse of rage in my family. Because Dad was no longer able, I felt I was being called to go to the nursing home and pray over him, taking authority over that curse so that it could not continue through the coming generations.

Dad was now 101 years old and living in a long term care facility. Having lost the ability to walk, he was now in a wheelchair, unable to speak with clarity and most often confused. He hated his condition, and in his own way made it abundantly clear he wanted to go home to heaven. My mom had died two years before, and he missed her.

I had power of attorney over all his affairs so felt God telling me I also had the spiritual authority to do this, as Dad was unable to at this point in his life. But could I do this? Would he be frightened, angry, or insulted? And what if the staff walked in? I wrestled with God all day, begging for a release from this assignment. But the feeling only surged relentlessly. What good was writing about spiritual warfare if I wasn't going to be obedient myself in this area?

By late afternoon, I'd put down my books, grabbed some cookies, jumped into my lime green Volkswagen Beetle and headed across town to pray over my dad!

When I arrived, Dad's smile said he'd been waiting for me. I made him a small coffee and fed him the shortbread cookies, then watched in amazement as his head dropped to his chest. He was sound asleep!

"Lord, is it okay if I do this while he is sleeping?" I felt God's grace and mercy giving me permission. So I began to pray, inviting the Holy Spirit to fill the tiny room and protect us. I asked forgiveness for my dad, then, speaking out loud, stood my ground, took authority I'd been given, and in the power of the name of Jesus, I told the generational spirit of anger and rage that time was up. It was not allowed to continue working in this family anymore. It must leave and go to the feet of Jesus of Nazareth, who would deal with him. Then I asked the Holy Spirit to fill the space where this spirit had resided.

I was amazed at how smoothly this had gone, but then a strange thing happened as my dad slept on. That one small cup of coffee he drank began to pour out of his mouth. It kept on coming until he was soaked, his shoes were filled, and the floor was completely covered. At least four cups of coffee flowed from him and kept on coming. All I could do was stand and watch! When the deluge finally stopped, my dad slowly lifted his head, opened his eyes, looked right at me, and said with complete clarity, "Oh hello, dear. When did you get here, and what were you doing?"

I took a look at the massive mess, removed my hand from his head, and just said, "I was praying over you, Dad."

"Well, thank you. That's always a good thing to do." The first few coherent sentences I had heard my dad say in months! I knew a God thing had just happened, and I was so glad I'd been obedient.

My dad died four months later, but he seemed different the last few months of his life—less agitated and more at peace.

That day gave me a glimpse into God's desire to bring spiritual freedom from the bondage of darkness, at any stage of life! He wants us delivered of evils we may not even realize have settled in. Like my experience earlier that week, what seem like simple rights are far more sinister, and their vicious grip seeks to keep us captive.

When I got home from visiting my dad, I retrieved my computer from under my desk, blew off the dust, cracked my rusty knuckles, and started writing what I was learning about this amazing journey called spiritual warfare.

Questions

Have you encountered evil in a tangible way? If so, when? How did it make you feel? How did you respond?

When have you heard from God about something He wanted you to deal with in your life? Did you do it? Share or write about that experience.

Are you willing to ask God, "What do you want to show me that I need to confess? Is there someone I need to forgive?" Why don't you do that right now? Take a pen and paper and ask God those questions. Then sit quietly as you wait to hear what He will reveal. Get ready to start writing!

Thinking back, do you feel there may be a generational curse in your family? Can you write about that or share it with someone who can pray with you?

Has this chapter called you to action in any way? How?

Chapter Ten
Taking Authority

My little granddaughter stepped softly past the dining room door, then took a step back and peered in. It was empty. She let out a sigh of relief and carried on to the kitchen, where I sat having tea and chatting with my daughter, her mom. We were talking about spiritual warfare and the unwanted presence of evil. Things had happened in their home that made my daughter wonder if it needed to be prayed through again.

I looked at my granddaughter's sweet face and for some reason asked her, "Honey, have you ever seen anything appear in *your* room that scared you?"

She quietly thought for a moment, then said, "Well, not in my room, but...in the dining room sometimes I saw a family. There was a mother and a father and a girl about my age. They were dressed kind of old-fashioned, and the little girl looked like she was very sick. Her eyes were dark and her face was sad."

"Oh my," I said, "that must have been scary for you! What were they doing?"

"Well, they were always just standing there, looking right at me. They didn't say anything, but I could tell they were not real people, kinda like spirits in a way. I drew a sketch of them in my drawing book. I'll go get it."

As she ran off to find her book, I felt energy rise up within me. I knew from experience with one of my sons that apparitions appear to children with no other apparent purpose than to terrify them. Children are our most defenseless members, and the roaring lion, Satan, often seeks to attack the weakest.

She returned quickly and presented an excellent drawing of the dining room visitors. "Sweetheart," I leaned forward in my chair to get closer to her, "Do you know if you just say, 'In the name of Jesus, get out!' that they will have to leave?"

"Yes," she calmly said, "Mommy told me that. And the next time I saw them, I said those words and they disappeared. I haven't seen them again." Her face was serene, and I just wanted to kiss that sweet thing. She'd already learned to take authority over evil and experienced the power of God to deliver her from that presence. My darling granddaughter learned a scriptural truth that so many of us either don't know or are afraid to act upon.

Isn't this story encouraging? Seeing a child take the gift of authority with faith and confidence in God's power and see deliverance should spur us on!

But it's important to understand authority.

Authority by definition is "the power or right to give orders, make decisions, and enforce obedience." It is also the right to act in a specified way, delegated from one person or organization to another. Another way of saying this is the power given to someone by another to control, command, or determine an action.

So *spiritual* authority is this: the right God gives to Christians, through the power of the name of Jesus and His blood shed on the cross, to give orders to Satan and his dark angels, in accordance to and in line with the Holy Word of God.

This authority comes from our relationship with Christ Jesus (see chapter three). It has no reflection on our feelings or emotions, which can both mislead, nor is it from any power in ourselves. Authority also has nothing to do with our personality type or character, earthly importance, or skill set. It is a gift from Jesus, through His Holy Spirit, for all those who have put their faith in Him. We are given authority the moment we become children of God. Spiritual authority is entrusted to us, and God's wisdom helps us manage it.

We are to treat this gift as something of value—something precious. We don't own authority or consider it our right to do whatever we choose. Nor have we any authority over God or the ability to make Him do our will. We are taking a stand allowed by God, through His power over the enemy, period.

Jesus gave authority to His disciples on more than one occasion (Matthew 28:18, Luke 9:1,2). While on earth, Jesus received His power from the Holy Spirit, and He passed this on to His disciples to do the same things He was doing, ultimately giving power and authority to all Christians coming after. John 14:12 *"Very truly I tell you, whoever believes in me will do the works I have been doing, and they will do even greater things than these, because I am going to the Father."*

God-given authority over evil is for all Christians who will accept it!

Now I would be remiss if I didn't stop here and share an unusual point of view. One of my favorite Bible professors was an incredible man named Erwin Lutzer. Back then he was just Mr. Lutzer. Now, he is Dr. Lutzer, Pastor Emeritus of The Moody Church in Chicago where he served for thirty-five years.

Erwin Lutzer was able to turn our short class into the most amazing journey through Scripture. When he spoke at chapel or Sunday service, he simply held a small Bible in his hand, with a finger placed somewhere between the pages, and drew us in to a spiritual journey without looking at a note or referencing the verses he recited. His teaching flowed from a deep relationship with God, and it inspired within me the desire to know more. Needless to say, I have read many of his published works and am still in awe of his knowledge. It is from his book *God's Devil* that I must share an important concept.[9]

God is not wringing His hands in heaven, wondering what to do with His fallen angel, Lucifer. He knew before creating him that he would sin and be cast from heaven, yet created him anyways, because God can still use Satan's evil ultimately for good. Whatever evil the devil is up to, God has allowed it for a purpose, even though we may not see it fulfilled in our lifetime.

God watches Satan's every move and is in complete control at all times. Throughout Scripture we see how God allows Satan just enough rope to hang himself, but there is always a divine purpose behind it. The devil's days are numbered, and when God has no more use for him, he will be cast into the lake of fire prepared for him and his followers.

But for now, Dr. Lutzer reminds us Satan is just a hapless player in the drama that he himself set in motion. Remembering that God is using Satan to do His mighty

---

[9] Lutzer, *God's Devil.*

will, we will tread more carefully through the next portion of this book and keep this knowledge always before us as we talk about taking authority over this evil being. Only through the permission of Almighty God do we move forward and see deliverance. The devil must obey God, and if our spoken word, even in the name of Jesus, does not move him, it could be because God has a different plan. Regardless, we need to know that through our redemption, we have been given a portion of authority over the devil, and with God's approval, we must take our stand and stand our ground.

There are several types of authority shown throughout the Bible: spousal authority, pastoral authority, gift-based authority, general Christian authority, and permission-based authority. Authority is almost always given to confront and bind evil and speak deliverance and freedom from that source of bondage.

Julie Marquis is a gifted counselor and writer in a deliverance ministry. She says that a huge challenge arises when we humans have issues with authority and submission to those over us. That struggle indicates a heart issue of rebellion. Rebelling against authority is actually rebelling against Christ, and this needs to be dealt with before there can be healing and restoration.

Spousal authority often pushes buttons and triggers for us women. The premise of husbands being the head of the household and in a position of authority over their wives comes from 1 Peter 3:1-7 ESV. Spiritual authority has a hierarchy in this situation. The husband has the greatest spiritual authority power in his household, assuming he is a godly man and living in obedience to Scripture. His position, given to him by the living God, is to spiritually stand in front of his wife and family as a guard and protector. When husbands and fathers take a stand against spiritual forces, their prayers are powerful. One quickly spoken prayer can instantly bring results. Unfortunately, not all husbands are believers in this process. Sometimes a husband isn't even a Christian and does not have that authority over Satan. In this case, the highest authority is given to the believing wife and mother. She then has the power to deal with evil as it shows up, knowing there will be God-given victory. But if both hearts are in acceptance with God's plan, amazing, miraculous things happen in that home and relationship.

Different positions hold spiritual authority. My pastor has spiritual authority over our church family. Authority is also given to a leader or founder of an organization. As Executive Director, I have spiritual authority over our mission in Haiti. Gord, my husband, has spiritual authority over me. When our children were young, we both had spiritual authority over them. My youngest son, TJ, started a company that builds custom-designed sheds. He has spiritual authority over that business and his staff as they work under him. A good friend now directs and runs a Christian camp. He has spiritual authority over that camp and all who come in under his leadership. Mothers have authority over their children and others within their home. When we have grandchildren under our care, we have spiritual authority over them.

Sometimes we find ourselves in a situation where we know we do not have scripturally based authority. If we are the only one available to do the job at hand, we can ask God to give us temporary, or permission-based authority.

An example of this, if you remember, was the time I was called to pray over my dad and bind a generational curse.

That was God-directed permission-based authority. But others can give us authority over them as well.

I was visiting my daughter and her children one afternoon, when my six-year-old grandson came running downstairs saying he knew there was someone in his closet because the doorknob was turning back and forth. My daughter was busy with a new baby, so I asked her for authority to go pray over his room, bind any spirit that may have taken up residence, and command it to leave. She gladly gave permission, saying out loud, "I give you the authority to pray over my son and his room," and I went, fully equipped to handle that situation. Once in the bedroom, I said, "If there is any spirit here not of God, I'm commanding you in the name of Jesus to get out." My grandson was significantly calmer as we went downstairs, and as far as I know, that doorknob has not suspiciously moved again.

Another example of permission-based authority is when Jesus gave the disciples authority to overcome the power of the enemy as they went out to preach (Matthew 28:18).

Although we understand the concept of having authority given by God, there is something important we need to remember.

As women, especially mothers, we are used to making decisions quickly, taking control of a situation and using our position to exert our authority over our kids, our family, and perhaps even elderly parents under our care. This can be problematic for us in the area of spiritual warfare. If we view it the same as we do running the household, it can become a matter of *control* for us instead of a call to obedience.

One day at our mission in Haiti, I was sitting under a palm tree having my devotions and prayer before the staff arrived and the day got busy. I had been praying for my children and grandchildren as I do each day, when God stopped me. I understood Him to say to me, "Heather, you are praying answers. You are telling Me what you want Me to do for your family. Your controlling grasp is keeping Me from doing the things I want to do. What *I* want is for you to start praying the will of heaven over them, loosing the purpose and plan I created them for. Bring Me your requests, but with open hands, accepting My will as good, acceptable and perfect."

I have to admit the tears began to flow as I realized that was exactly what I had been doing. As a mom of six, I'd been forced to be the "problem fixer" for years, making quick decisions and changes, but this would not work spiritually. Praying changed for me that day as I realized I had been trying to control God instead of asking Him to control me, and my family. Now, I pray God's perfect plan and will over each one of my twenty-six precious children and grandchildren and, at the same time, pray over those yet to come.

There can be danger in trying to control the enemy as well. If there is any question of authority, instead of jumping into this full-blown war on another's behalf, we should stop and ask permission from God. Very seldom have I sensed a "no," but checking with God first about anything we do in the spiritual realm is not wasted time. It focuses our eyes on the living God and His power, instead of ourselves and what we want to do. God blesses that.

Now, if we are dealing with spiritual interference in our own life, I believe we already have God's permission. We don't need to ask. We have it. If there is something I feel needs to be dealt with, such as a thought, a presence, an illness, an attitude, or a problem, I usually say, "If this is not of God, in the power of the name of Jesus, I command you to get out and leave me alone!" It is quite amazing how that pesky spirit instantly lets go and is gone.

Many times while working on this manuscript, I would be overcome with a fit of coughing, choking, hiccups, or a barrage of sneezing. It was disruptive to my work, and I would lose my train of thought, unable to finish a sentence. I'd finally speak up, saying, "If this is you, Satan, trying to destroy this process, in the name of Jesus, stop it!" There would not be one more cough, hiccup, or sneeze, and I could continue in peace.

One night, after working on a particularly difficult chapter, I could not sleep for debilitating foot cramps. I tried to walk them off, but my feet were painfully twisting and I couldn't continue. Gord offered to rub them but that made it worse. I suddenly remembered what I'd been working on that day, and a light bulb moment revealed the source. In a very annoyed voice, I said, "If these cramps are not from You, Lord, I'd like to bind whatever is causing them. In the name of Jesus Christ, my Creator and healer, I'm telling you, Satan, to get out of my feet!"

Instantly...instantly, the muscles relaxed and my feet returned to normal. Pain and cramping were gone. I went back to bed with words of praise in my heart for Jesus and this incredible gift of authority He gives.

So simple! So wonderful! Such a loving, powerful God!

When times like this happen and God reveals the source, we know He is calling us to take a stand. Permission has already been given for us to act.

Accepting authority is a learning curve, a journey, and a process, but we need to start somewhere. I believe this very moment is the time. Stepping up to the task is going to be as unique as *we* are.

For some, it will be as easy as grabbing our favorite color of lipstick in the morning and applying it. For others, it will be like breaking in a new pair of shoes, slowly, cautiously, and carefully, but in the end the result is the same. (No, not blisters!) It will become a comfortable, automatic response, done as easily as Jesus calming the wind and the waves. It will bring victory. It will give freedom. What a wonderful gift!

I must add a warning here. I have learned that unless we have dealt with sin in our life, especially unforgiveness, resentment or bitterness toward another, Satan feels his invitation to be there has not really been revoked. He still has a right to torment us. It is only when we've confessed, repented and renounced these sins that we're given that right to take authority over evil.

Satan and his kingdom of dark angels and demons must acknowledge and respect the places of authority God has set up. It is non-negotiable for him. When people in places of authority take a stand, stand their ground, and stand in the powerful name of Jesus of Nazareth, Satan looks at us and finds himself before Almighty God. He has no choice but to obey.

Gift-based authority

The gifts of the Holy Spirit by nature open opportunities to us. As we discover our spiritual gifts and use them to glorify God, He gives us the ability to discern evil and take our stand against it. This can look as different as each spiritual gift given. Keep going, my friend. There will be more about this in chapter twelve.

Questions

Have you or any of your children had an experience of seeing spirits in your home? If you're not sure, you may want to talk to your kids and gently find out if this has happened to them. You may be surprised at their answer.

How do you feel about the concept that God allows the devil to work evil, in accordance with His purposes? Can you think of an instance in your life where something Satan may have wanted for harm actually brought about something good in your life? Perhaps a healing, a revelation, a bad habit to deal with or a change needed in a relationship? If so, write about it.

Is control an issue for you? How could this change your prayer life concerning yourself or your family? Record your response to this revelation in a journal or write a daily prayer you can read that reveals a submissive heart to God's perfect will.

How do you feel about taking the authority God gives you when He reveals a situation that requires Satan to be rebuked?

Will accepting God's hierarchy of authority in families be an issue for you? Are you willing to pray right now asking God to give you the grace and willingness to accept it?

Chapter Eleven
Praying with Power

I was bone weary as I crawled into the vehicle. It had been several long, exhausting months. We were saying goodbye to the last work team for the year visiting our mission in Haiti, and were heading home ourselves. Many volunteers had come to help, and although several projects had been completed and hundreds of hungry children had been fed, the past week had been fraught with problems, and my husband and I were tired and ready to get back to Canada. Christmas preparations would be in full swing when we returned and that meant precious family time—something we dearly missed working so many miles away. Those weeks would pass quickly though, and before we knew it, it would be time to head back to Haiti once again...so we were anxious to be on our way.

The journey from our mission compound to the airport in Port au Prince is long and often dangerous. It's certainly not for the faint of heart, and has been known to cause a shudder through the most steadfast soul. Yes, driving in Haiti is an adventure!

The few traffic lights in the capital city are often moved around in hopes someone will actually stop for the red, but usually to no avail, making intersections jumbled confusion and terrifying close calls. While traffic on these pothole-infused roads is always heavy, there are also no speed limits or rules. Anyone can pass at anytime...even if all cars are already passing someone else. The narrow road could have four or five cars abreast...going in both directions and traveling at break neck speeds. Over the years we became somewhat numb to it, still, the 60-mile-long drive to the airport was always a concern.

My husband and I started this mission in 2006, and after several hair-raising events on the roads, we made a conscious decision to stop and pray before starting each journey across the country. But this particular trip home was quite different. Events that took place in the past week had called us to prayer as in no other time. Daily, we met as a team, in groups and in couples to petition God for His intervention in the difficult situations showing up each day. Prayer had almost become as regular for us as breathing and God had been gracious and merciful. We were heading home having seen His hand of power and provision.

Before the team piled into the van, we stood together, bowed our heads, and asked for God's protection—specifically requesting angels to go before us and behind us; to keep us from dangers seen and unseen; to forbid the enemy from bringing harm on this journey in any way. Our son Peter was put in charge of the group in the van, while Gord and I and my cousin Dean climbed into a car with a Haitian driver. We were off.

As always, the roads that day were very busy, and we quickly lost sight of Pete and the team. Our chauffeur seemed quite anxious to get us through the traffic and to the airport on time, so we moved swiftly down the bone-jarring highway. Swerving around Taptaps—old half-ton trucks reconstructed to seat 25-30 passengers on benches with live goats and chickens hanging from the sides—passing motorbike taxis with families of four or five on board, and the occasional beat-up school bus stuffed with passengers inside as well as piled high on the roof.

Suddenly, we found ourselves behind an extremely large truck pulling a long flatbed trailer. Swaying on top of the trailer directly in front of us was a monstrous machine. Through the layers of caked-on mud peeked the largest road grader we had ever seen. Its dimensions took up the entire width of the road, and with steady on-coming traffic there was no way around it, even for our anxious driver. Although the gigantic machine did not seem to be safely secured, we had no choice but to tuck in behind it and wait for an opportunity to pass.

Conversation between the three of us had come to an abrupt end as we focused on the unsteady piece of equipment. It pitched and swayed back and forth, the chains that supposedly secured it flopping dangerously about. Suddenly, there was an ear-splitting explosion. Frozen in our seats, we watched two huge back tires blow off the flat bed trailer to become deadly air-born projectiles headed straight for our front windshield, and in that spit second, knew we were looking death in the face.

Then the unimaginable happened.

At the last second before striking our windshield, as though blocked by an unseen hand, one tire veered off to the right side of our car, whizzing past Dean's window, and the other tire swerved around the left side, flashing past my husband's. The force of them was so powerful and close we could feel the gust of wind rock our vehicle, and smell the burning rubber as they flew past. A glimpse through the back window revealed the massive, wayward tires bursting into flames on opposite sides of the road. And for just a moment, I thought I heard the gentle rush of angel's wings.

We carried on in silence until my husband finally said, "Did that really just happen?"

Still unable to speak, I could do nothing more than nod my head.

There was no denying we had just experienced a miracle, being walked through the valley of the shadow of death. That simple, yet heart-felt prayer before we left had been answered in a most miraculous way. God heard from heaven, sent His angels, and we all lived to see another day.

Although it had become almost a ritual to pray for protection, we had never really expected to see it answered in the form of a visible miracle. In retrospect, I wonder if God decided that day to show us an example of his mighty power to increase our faith and assure our dependence on Him in the future. If so, it worked.

Praying now has a new authenticity for us, a greater necessity and even urgency, and today we feel as never before, our very lives depend on it.

That story always makes me think of Philippians 4:6,7, "*Do not be anxious about anything, but in every situation by prayer and petition, with thanksgiving, present your requests to God. And the peace of God which surpasses all understanding, will guard your heart and your mind in Christ Jesus.*"

I've heard it said, "Earth waits for heaven to act, but heaven waits for earth to ask." We read in James 4:2, "*You do not have because you do not ask.*" Even when we look at the healing miracles of Jesus in the New Testament, we see He seldom initiated them, but was usually responding to those asking, begging, or pleading Him for it.

We often think the purpose of prayer is to let God know what we need and to get Him to take care of it for us, providing and protecting. But the primary purpose of prayer is actually quite different. It's to *align our thoughts, our actions and our life with the perfect will of God*. Sometimes, like the week prior to our exploding tire adventure, our prayers need to be more about asking for help to get *through* difficult times than asking to get *out* of them.

Our son Peter is an incredible fine woodworker. Pieces he has worked on have ended up in Canadian embassies around the world. He has the creativity and skill to produce beautiful works of art, and has told me an important part of the process is the finishing. He works for weeks just sanding and rubbing different oils in for a beautiful finish that helps set the piece apart from any other.

God often uses challenges and difficulties to sandpaper us into something more beautiful and refined—something He can use for His glory. Sometimes He needs to start with a coarse grade sandpaper to change our bent and twisted spiritual condition. Sometimes He just uses a finer grade to smooth out a stubborn area, but blending our will to His is always the ultimate goal.

And those beautiful oils and surface treatments Pete uses make me think of the Holy Spirit who then works in and through us to create a beautiful finish to God's masterpiece, setting us apart for His divine purpose.

Sad news is, we will never be perfect. Good news is, God knows that, but our repentant prayers allow God to move us through the mistakes we make, to use us in our imperfect state.

Prayer from an open heart ushers us into the presence of a mighty God who hears our every word. It can bring forgiveness and healing, making us ready to be realigned, ready for His service, and ready to see miracles.

Simplicity

For some, praying is a foreign activity. Perhaps not being raised in a praying home has left you with uneasiness about talking to God. How do we talk to someone we cannot see? And how do we approach such a powerful being with our simple thoughts and vocabulary? Will He hear our humble words? Will He see our desperation? Or will He turn away from our awkwardness like anyone else would?

Regardless of our fears, praying is essential. To not pray is like telling God we are fine on our own and don't need Him. To never pray is not only disobedient, it is arrogant. Not praying eliminates one side of the conversation, and all worthy relationships require both talking and listening. Yes, praying is most essential!

God speaks clearly throughout Scripture about prayer and gives us a perfect example in Luke 11:1-23, which we can pray anytime. But there is more.

He wants us to speak our heart. He wants us in simple, yet earnest words to tell Him what we need and what we long for. He wants to hear what is breaking our hearts, what we are sorry for, what is frightening us, and what we are grateful for. He is glorified when we express our love and worship, declaring His greatness, His beauty, His goodness, and His majesty.

To put it simply, He just wants us to talk to Him, in whatever way we are able, in whatever words we have, about whatever we need to tell or ask Him. There is no magic formula or specific education needed.

In Haiti, we welcome many visitors to the Hope Grows Haiti mission compound. They come to do medical work, mission work, teaching, pastoral training, and building projects. With each team arriving, we have an orientation night, laying out the week and our rules and practices. One thing we make clear is that we pray over everything. In fact, we don't even leave the compound without stopping at the gate and praying for protection.

Not all teams are Christians, but all come with hearts filled with a longing to serve in a less privileged country. They get used to us praying all the time but don't really understand why.

One morning I took a group to visit new babies in the village. We stopped at the gate to pray. "Dear Jesus," I said, "please give us angels to go before us and behind us, protecting us from biting dogs, rolled ankles, overflowing riverbanks, and falling mangoes." There were a few snickers as I continued my petition, then I said amen. Immediately a monster mango torpedoed like a cannon ball down through the branches of a massive tree beside us, exploding in the dust at our feet. Everyone jumped, gasped, then fell silent. Someone behind me whispered, "Wow. Now I see why we pray!"

God has a sense of humor, and I believe He wanted this group to have a glimpse of how He works. The team had just seen the hand of God in answer to a very simple prayer. I must add that each time we approached the gates after that, someone always asked, "Are we going to pray?"

Psalm 9:9,10 *"The Lord is a refuge for the oppressed, a stronghold in times of trouble. Those who know Your name trust in You, for You, LORD, have never forsaken those who seek you."*

One thing that has helped many learn to pray is using the acronym **ACTS** as a step-by-step process through prayer:

Adoration—praise and worship either in words or song to begin our time with the Lord.

Confession—here we ask God to search us and cleanse us of any unconfessed sins. If we also use this time to listen for prompting from the Holy Spirit, He'll often bring to mind things we may not be aware of. Then we are able to repent of whatever is revealed.

Thanksgiving—count your blessings! Expressing gratefulness for all the blessings in our life reminds us that, *"all good gifts come from above, coming down from the Father of lights"* (James 1:17). Taking time to name them has an even deeper effect on our spirit, bringing greater appreciation.

Supplication—this is another word for asking. James 4:2 says, *"You have not because you ask not."* So let's ask!

God already knows what we need and what we are going to ask for. He knows everything! We don't surprise Him with our requests, but He wants us to acknowledge His gracious gift giving, and spit out what it is we'd like Him to do. Matthew 6:32 refers to many of the things that cause us concern. *"For the pagans run after all these things, but your heavenly Father knows that you need them."*

God wants us to come to Him, to ask Him, to thank Him. He is a good, understanding, loving Father, but He wants us to make the effort. He hears and understands the shortest prayer, the hesitant prayer, the humble prayer, and the desperate prayer.

I will never forget Alice's story and the prayer that changed her hopelessly tragic situation.

I met Alice in 2012, three weeks after the devastating earthquake in Haiti. I was visiting elderly in our town who had been left homeless and without the food and water needed to survive. We carried as much with us as we could while struggling through crumbled ruins and slimy mud pits from recent rains. I spotted Alice sitting on the ground outside a tiny, severely leaning hut, caressing a tattered, open Bible with soiled, wrinkled hands. Her blindness was evident, and when I reached for her hand to give her a piece of bread and peanut butter, she pulled me toward her with surprising strength and began to pray out loud, thanking God profusely (with a cascade of Creole and intermittent hallelujahs) for sending someone to bring her food and a drink of water. She knew where this gift had actually come from, and it wasn't me! This food had arrived in answer to a prayer. After finishing every speck of sustenance, she asked us to sit so she could share her story. I'll never forget her words. They touched my heart, and I know her story will touch yours too.

Many years ago Alice's husband went to visit his family, asking for a small piece of their land, enough so they could build a home to live in and have a garden to raise vegetables to sell and eat. He did not return, so after several days Alice went to find him.

As she approached the house, neighbors called to her and told her the family had killed her husband and buried him somewhere. She was distraught, and began banging on the family's door. It opened suddenly, and her husband's brothers grabbed her. They dragged her across the property to an abandoned well and threw her in. She landed hard, her legs crumpling beneath her. Alice cried out with pain. The next thing she knew, rocks were being thrown down upon her. When a large one connected with her head, there was a loud crack. She was instantly blind.

Calling for them to stop met with laughter, then dirt rained down, choking her as it buried her alive. She struggled to breathe through the dirt and dust.

The two men left her for dead, and she lay in the well throughout the night, struggling to dig a space about her to let in fresh air. As early morning light streamed into the dark well, Alice knew she was dying. She had been raised in voodoo, worshipping Satan and aware of that dark spirit's evil ways, but she knew he would not be able to help her. It had to be a greater spirit.

Then Alice remembered hearing a missionary tell about the strong God called Jesus and how He loved every person. She gathered breath in her burning lungs. "Jesus," her raspy voice wavered, "help me!"

A Christian woman on her way to market was walking past at that moment and heard that feeble plea come from the well. She called down to Alice to hold on and ran to get help.

Within a few moments, someone was lowered into the well and began digging her out. He put ropes around her so others could lift her out and then carried Alice to a mission for healing and recovery. They cleaned and fed her, gave her clothes to wear, and taught her about the Jesus she had called upon. Over the following days, these kind Samaritans showed her how to accept Him into her life.

Jesus heard a simple prayer from the heart of an uneducated, unloved, broken woman—and answered. Because of that, Alice lived thirty more years telling others about the One who had changed her life. She shared with all who would listen that God sees, God hears, and God answers prayer.

Alice's desperate prayer reminds me of Jonah's words in chapter 2, verse 2. *"I cried out to the Lord in my distress, and He answered me!"* God rescued Jonah, just like He rescued my friend Alice, and He can rescue us too!

Alice died in 2016 but will always be remembered for her joyful spirit and heart of thanksgiving to the One who rescued her from a deep dark pit. My last image of Alice is at our mission as we lifted our hearts to God in prayer during a service. While we prayed, Alice felt her way off the chair to lower her swollen knees onto the rough concrete in reverence to the God who heard her first prayer. Alice loved God.

And God loved Alice!

When we see how three simple words prayed in earnest were heard and miraculously answered, we can have confidence that our ordinary words will be heard too. Whether in the morning when we are fresh or in the middle of the night when we are kept awake by fears and troubles, God is always listening.

Psalm 5:23 *"Listen to my voice in the morning, Lord. Each morning I bring my requests to You and wait expectantly."*

Lamentations 2:19 *"Rise during the night and cry out! Pour out your hearts like water to the Lord. Lift up your hands to Him in prayer, pleading for your children."*

God hears our prayers. All of them. There will be times when our prayers take on specific purpose and urgency, while other times our prayers will be quite different, perhaps filled with praise and thanksgiving or confession and repentance. God gives us the gift of prayer, and the Holy Spirit directs our words and thoughts as we allow. Many times we will feel called to pray Scripture, speaking back to God His words of promise or encouragement. Perhaps verses that express longing for His presence, or His worship and adoration come to mind, and we repeat them as from our own heart. God loves to hear that.

Divinely directed prayer can be quite varied in form.

Divinely directed prayer

• Praying over family

Prayer is a gracious gift God gives to wives and mothers. No one knows our kids and husbands as well as we do. No one hears hidden meaning between words spoken, and understands the reason behind it, like a mom. No one cares about our kids' hurting hearts like we do. No one wants the very best for a family like a wife and mother. We see their potential, we see their faults, we know their vulnerabilities and propensity for disaster. We believe they are created for a purpose and want so much for it to be fulfilled. A godly woman's greatest desire is for her family to walk in faith and live in victory.

God's gift of prayer has provided a way for us to speak those private things of our heart and know we have been heard. But we need to remember, in this age of instant gratification, God's answer will always be in His perfect timing. Perhaps not in our timing, but His giving will always be rich with blessing.

Matthew 7:9-11 *"Which of you [moms], when your child asks for bread, will give them a stone? Or if they ask for fish, will give them a snake? If you then, though you are evil, know how to give good gifts to your children, how much more will your Father in heaven give good gifts to those who ask Him?"*

I love the thought that the prayers of loved ones gone before us remain before the Father, filling a bowl of sweet smelling incense as it fills up and tips out with God's grace, mercy, and blessings in answer to the petitions prayed. I come from a legacy of rich prayer warriors and anticipate the answers yet to come, also knowing my prayers for generations to come will be answered in God's perfect time and way.

If this is not your heritage, then it's time to start one. There is no better day than today. As our children hear us praying, watch us praying over them, and see the hand of God as He answers, it will give them great motivation in their own prayer life. That tradition is one worth passing on.

Joel 1:3 *"Tell your children of it, and let your children tell their children, and their children to another generation."*

A great resource for this topic is *Praying Circles Around the Lives of Your Children* by Mark Batterson.[10]

---

[10] Mark Batterson, *Praying Circles Around the Lives of Your Children.* Zondervan, 2014.

• Intercessory prayers

Intercessory prayer is bold, it is stubborn, and it is often desperate. This type of prayer is always for another, and many times it comes upon us with urgency. One night that call pressed in on me.

As I floated somewhere between asleep and awake, a scene played out in my mind. I saw my daughter Becki walking down the side of a highway in the dark. Her car had broken down, and she left it behind on the side of the road. A large transport truck pulled up beside her, the passenger door opening and a voice within offering a ride. She climbed in, shut the door, and disappeared into the night.

I jolted to a sitting position, sweating and terrified. The clock showed it was midnight. Becki should be home by now. Running into her room, I saw the bed empty and instantly knew that it was not just a dream, but a message from God. My daughter was in jeopardy, and I was being called to pray—and pray earnestly. I prayed the blood of Jesus over her, quoted Scripture, and offered praise and petition for two hours. At 2:00am, I saw headlights drive up our long driveway and peered with my nose pressed to the window as my daughter crawled out of a strange car. When she came through the door, I was waiting with joyful tears and a long, tight hug.

After sharing my experience with her, I learned my dream was exactly what had happened. The only difference between what I saw and what actually happened, was when the driver slowed down to stop, instead of taking Becki, he started up again and drove away. Then another car with a mother and daughter, who were driving past, saw what was happening, were concerned, and turned around to pick her up and bring her safely home.

I believe that intercessory prayer brought an angel for Becki, one who signaled the truck driver to keep on going while whispering to that mother to come back and pick her up.

That night I witnessed the power of intercessory prayer, and will never forget it. I came to understand and appreciate its importance in a totally new way.

There may not always be as dramatic an event, but there will always be a powerful purpose for the calling. I have a lot of children and have been called to intercessory prayer in many ways. Sometimes it's for healing, sometimes for wisdom, peace, discernment, a passion for scripture, or just knowledge of God's presence through a difficult day. At times I have been called to pray against a revelation of demonic attack. It is a full-time responsibility I take seriously.

While sitting at my dressing table one morning, I looked down and noticed a business card. It had been given to me from a friend a few years earlier. I wasn't sure why, but I instantly felt called to pray for her. So I did. Every morning when I put on my makeup, I looked at that card and prayed God's protection and blessing over her, still not knowing why, just that I must.

It continued for a couple of months then I heard some sad news. Over the two months I had been praying, her life had taken a terrible turn. My friend and her husband were living in Mexico when she became very sick and was taken to hospital. My dear friend recovered, but her husband picked up the vicious corona virus while visiting her, and died. She had not been allowed to be with him and had to let him go without holding his hand, telling him she loved him, or saying goodbye. I finally connected with her later to see how she was doing. She assured me God had walked through this tragedy with her. She had felt His love and presence holding her. The sadness was great, but the comforting hand of her loving God had gently softened the ragged edges of grief.

I know I was not the only one called to pray for this friend, but what a powerful reminder for me to be obedient in the call, even if I don't know the purpose.

An excellent resource on this topic is *The Secrets of Intercessory Prayer* by Jack Hayford.[11]

• Prayers of thanksgiving and worship
Psalm 100:1,4 *"Shout for joy to the LORD, all the earth. Worship the LORD with gladness: come before him with joyful songs. Enter His gates with thanksgiving and his courts with praise; give thanks to him and praise his name."*

Attitude is always a choice. We tell our kids that. God tells us that. Scripture encourages good attitudes...especially one of thanksgiving, which also comes with a promise!

A spirit of gratitude allows the heart-grip of struggles to lessen, and we can see life from a different perspective. We stop focusing on ourselves and turn our thoughts to God. We see the good things God has done in and for us, and we approach Him with greater humility. We stop to remember how good and gracious He is. It is hard to remain angry or self absorbed when we are truly giving thanks.

---

[11] Jack Hayford, *The Secrets of Intercessory Prayer.* Chosen Books, 2012.

Coming before Almighty God with hearts filled with praise, worship, and gratitude moves us to be respectful, more aware of His continuous goodness, and willing to accept His perfect will.

A grateful heart changes us before we ever get to the asking.

Worship also moves us into a space where God can reveal unconfessed sin in our life. We have seen how sin is sneaky and tries to hide in the deep recesses of our heart. God wants to expose those sins.

David said in Psalm 139:23-24, "*Search me oh God, and know my heart; test me and know my anxious thoughts. See if there is any offensive way in me, and lead me in the way everlasting.*"

When we pray this prayer of David, God often brings shocking attitudes and thoughts to mind, giving us a chance to repent and renounce them. This daily prayer assures us of standing before the living God with a clean heart, ready to receive what He wants to give.

Even more than that, gratitude steals Satan's thunder! We are much less apt to fall for his prompting of selfish ambition, selfishness, and self-pity when we are expressing thankfulness and worship to God. Demons will tremble at our prayers, because they know this attitude touches the heart of our Creator and invites Him into our hopes and desires. That leaves the devil *out!*

Hebrews 12:28-29 "*Therefore, since we are receiving a kingdom that cannot be shaken, let us be thankful, and so worship God acceptably with reverence and awe, for our God is a consuming fire.*"

If you are looking for more on this topic, Joyce Meyer has written a devotional, *The Power of Being Thankful.*[12]

• Authority prayer

We are told in Ephesians 6:12 that *"Our struggle is not against flesh and blood, but against rulers, authorities, powers and spiritual forces of evil."* That means our enemy really isn't other people, it is Satan and his kingdom of darkness. Evil's purpose is to kill, steal, and destroy our life and that of our family.

Luke 9:1-2, tells us, *"When Jesus had called the twelve together, He gave them power and authority to drive out all demons and to cure diseases, and sent them out to proclaim the kingdom of God and to heal the sick."*

In Luke 10:19, Jesus says, *"I have given you authority to trample on snakes and scorpions and to overcome all the power of the enemy; nothing will harm you, however, do not rejoice that the spirits submit to you but rejoice that your names are written in heaven."*

Authority prayer is most often used in releasing and deliverance ministries, usually operated under a pastoral team through a Bible-teaching church, but also in personal experiences dealing with demonic beings.

Serious repentance and renouncing prayer is required before a releasing process, but there are times when we are given the knowledge and recognition of a demonic presence and understand we are to do something quickly. If we are not sure what exactly we're dealing with, we should qualify the command with "If this is not of God, in the name of Jesus

---

[12] Joyce Meyer, *The Power of Being Thankful.* FaithWords, 2014.

Christ and through His power, I command whatever spirit is behind this to leave." On rare occasions, we can speak to it without a doubt in our heart.

I have a few friends who serve as medical staff in psychiatric hospitals. We talk of the many cases where demonic forces are obviously at work in people in residence. The evidence is too real to ignore. One story shared with me exposes this truth in a powerful way.

Two police officers brought in an extremely combative man, slight in build but with the strength of ten men. Such strength required eight additional staff to hold the man down long enough to get restraints on him, keeping him from harming himself or others. Ten people could barely control this patient as he thrashed and cussed and clawed at them. Finally one of the officers simply said, "In the name of Jesus, leave him alone!" The combative man instantly slumped down in a silent and exhausted heap. His face turned slowly to the officer, and he weakly uttered, "Thank you."

That police officer knew the power of God and the loving heart of Jesus. He acted quickly, knowing the authority given to believers to call for deliverance and see the hand of God over the enemy.

There may also be times when we suspect a demonic presence but can't seem to find freedom from it. That is when we go right to God and ask Him to deal with the spirit that will not leave. Even Michael the archangel, when dealing with Satan over the body of Moses, prayed, *"May the Lord rebuke you!"* (Jude 1:9).

There are many books you can read on this topic but I would suggest *I Give You Authority* by Charles Kraft.[13]

• Prayer of repentance and confession

We did talk about this particular prayer in past chapters. It is a prayer that can be uttered every single day, when sin is detected, suspected, or reflected in our thoughts and actions. It is a prayer asking God for forgiveness when we falter. It is a prayer we pray in our heart or out loud, on our feet, on our knees or on our face before Him. It is a prayer that is usually followed with hearing from God, seeing God's hand, and experiencing that sweet, sweet peace He loves to give.

God hears and honors the prayer of confession. That prayer simply starts with, "Dear heavenly Father, please forgive me for..."

1 John 1:9 *"If we confess our sins, He is faithful and just and will forgive us our sins and purify us from **all** unrighteousness"* (emphasis added).

Reading through the Psalms and Proverbs reveals much more on this topic. I recommend taking a block of time to read through these two books of the Bible and write out or highlight the verses that touch your heart in a special, personal way.

• Listening prayer

There will be times when we feel God calling us to our "prayer closet"—a quiet, private place to go where there will be no interruptions. It may not be for any specific purpose other than to come before Him and listen.

---

[13] Charles Kraft, *I Give You Authority.* Chosen Books, 2012.

Psalm 62:1 MSG, *"God, the one and only—I'll wait as long as He says. Everything I need comes from Him, so why not?"*

Listening prayer is just that, listening. We take a note pad and pen into our prayer place and get on our knees. With an open heart, and an open Bible, we still our mind and body, ask God what it is He wants to tell us, and wait. The words, thoughts, or scriptures that come to mind should be written down, because the enemy will seek to steal God's message from our memory.

Messages from God could be words of encouragement, instruction, correction, or something He wants us to share. In the case of the latter, God will give us the name of the person with whom He wishes us to share His words.

I remember a specific quiet afternoon when God invited me to listening prayer. As the thoughts came, I wrote them as quickly and correctly as possible. It was lovely, but I wasn't sure they were for me. "God," I asked, "Who are these words for?" Immediately the face and name of our Field Director in Haiti came to mind.

I rose from my knees, picked up my phone, and sent that message to Wouillio, letting him know God had given it to me and I believed they were for him.

Five minutes later I received a message back. His sentences were punctuated with many exclamation marks. Wouillio said someone had prophesied those very words over him that morning, but he had asked God for confirmation. He was so excited to hear that message again and know every word of it was true!

God works in mysterious, miraculous ways!

Questions

Take a moment to think about your prayer life. Is it always the same? Are you praying answers? How would you like to change that interaction between you and God to develop a more powerful relationship and see specific answers?

Write out the primary purpose of prayer we discussed. How can you change the way you pray to reflect this?

Do you remember what the acronym ACTS stands for? Write it out here.

Have you ever been called to intercessory prayer on another's behalf? If not, ask God if there is someone He wants you to specifically pray for.

What answers to prayer have you seen in your lifetime? Share them with a family member or friend. Write about them in your journal. Thank God again for those times, and keep praying in faith to see the miracles God has waiting for you!

Chapter Twelve
The Gift of Gifts

Christmas morning always holds great excitement for me. As a kid, it was all about the presents—especially the ones for me. I know...how shallow! I would crawl from my bed in the early morning darkness and as noiselessly as possible get to the Christmas tree, which remained fully lit through the night. After gazing a moment at the glory of it all, I'd commence to squeeze, shake, sniff, and accidentally loosen some tape on the packages with my name. But I was almost as excited for my family to see what I had chosen to give them.

By the time I was eight, with my fifty-cent allowance in hand, I'd roam through Woolworths to find just the right objects for my brother, my mom, and my dad. It was often just a plastic comb for Ian, a doily for Mom, and a cheap pair of socks for Dad. Fifty cents went a long way back then! With careful wrapping and a big red bow, the gifts looked promising, and I could hardly wait for their reactions.

As it turns out, giving is one of my love languages, and to this day I enjoy watching my now extensive family open their gifts Christmas morning. I feel so much pleasure when I see them donning the jewelry, reading the book, digging in to the chocolate, or excited to try the new tool. I love the giving process, but seeing them use and enjoy their gifts gives me greater delight.

I imagine God is just a little bit like that when it comes to spiritual gifts. When He designed us, He also chose a spiritual gift perfect for us. He must be so pleased when we discover and use it the way He planned (see Romans 12, 1 Corinthians 12, 1 Peter 4, Ephesians 4).

Spiritual gifts are not usually for our own benefit but are to be used to serve others, bless the church, and bring God glory. It's exciting to know that the gifts given to the apostles so long ago are still given today. There is an abundance of evidence, writings, and experiences bearing that truth.

Spiritual gifts are often confused with natural gifts, which are qualities or talents apparent at an early age that continue developing over a lifetime—like music, athletics, artistic abilities, mechanics, technology, languages, or an incredible memory. These aptitudes are admirable and should be used to bring God glory, but they are not what Scripture refers to as spiritual gifts.

There is also the fruit of the Spirit listed in Galatians 5:22-23, which is different as well, and refers to qualities given when we become a child of God. When that happens, the Holy Spirit comes to live in us, bringing the gift of love, joy, peace, perseverance, kindness, goodness, faithfulness, gentleness, and self-control. All of these are for every Christian.

Spiritual gifts are unique to each of us, given by the Holy Spirit to perform a specific ministry that will build up the church body, encouraging and strengthening others. Bible scholars agree on defining gifting as three categories: love gifts, word gifts, and power gifts.

Twenty-one different gifts fall into these three parameters. All Christians have at least one, and most Christians have several.

The spiritual gift given to you was chosen by God before you were born. We need to be content in that, not wishing for some gift we see in another. That often develops into jealousy or dissatisfaction. Plus, it's a bit like telling God He doesn't know what He is doing.

Nor should we expect others to serve in an area that is not their gifting (an exception being the prompting of the Holy Spirit). It's so easy to pressure someone into a service they have not been called to, but if it is not in the area of their gift, there will be little joy on earth or in heaven in the performance. But when we are using the gift(s) God has given us to serve the church, we will feel complete, whole, and fulfilled.

The Bible talks about the church not as a building but as the family of believers—God's people—Christians in every village, city, and country. God's people are the body of the church, a precious yet imperfect one.

Because our gifts are to serve the church, we often feel we don't qualify for this and back away from learning which gifts are ours. But listen, we don't need to wait until we feel we have it all together before finding and using our spiritual gift, because that will probably never happen. God will use us just as we are, warts and all.

When my daughter Mandi and son Pete were teenagers, they decided to start a new Christmas tradition of their own. It was called the "best ugly wrapped gift." For several years in a row, they thought up ridiculous ways to present their gifts to each other. One year an old muddy rain boot hid the gift. Another year it was within a bag of household garbage, while another one involved a large container filled with Jell-O embracing the treasure. The wrapping was not beautiful and inspiring, but the gift inside was always worth the trouble. In a similar way, God never waits until we are perfect, organized, and put together to use our gifting (because He would be waiting forever). He uses us as we become willing and ready, and it will always bring about something worthwhile.

Romans 12:6-8 tells us, *"We have different gifts, according to the grace given to each of us. If your gift is prophesying, then prophesy in accordance with your faith; If it is serving, then serve; if it is teaching, then teach; if it is to encourage, then give encouragement; if it is giving, then give generously; if it is to lead, do it diligently; if it is to show mercy, do it cheerfully."*

No one gift is of greater value than another. All gifts are God given for the same purpose and have equal importance in the kingdom. Paul compares it all to a human body. The parts look different and have a different design, but they work together to do great things for the body as a whole!

Look at 1 Corinthians 12:21-25 in The Message. *"An enormous eye or a gigantic hand wouldn't be a body, but a monster. What we have is one body with many parts, each its proper size and in its proper place. No part is important on its own. Can you imagine Eye telling Hand, 'Get lost, I don't need you'? Or, Head telling Foot 'You're fired; your job has been phased out'? As a matter of fact, in practice it works the other way...the 'lower' the part, the more basic, and therefore necessary. You can live without an eye, for instance, but not without a stomach. When it's a part of your own body you are concerned with, it makes no difference whether the part is visible or clothed, higher or lower. You give it dignity and honor just as it is, without comparisons."*

The Spirit of God sees His people in the same way. All of us have an important place in God's family, and He gives many and varied gifts to many and varied believers, but they all work together to make the body whole, complete.

Each gift comes with a mandate—use it readily, cheerfully, and in unity. We will be held to account for how we have used the gift(s) given to us when we stand before Jesus. So let's learn what they are, which are ours, and get to it!

We'll go through the three categories: the love gifts, the word gifts, and the power gifts. As we do this, please be in prayer, asking God to reveal the one given to you.

Love gifts

Love gifts will show up in practical ways, like helps, mercy, giving, and administration.

After completing an online gifting quiz, one of the gifts revealed as mine was administration. I was shocked. I'm not too excited with administration, like filing, phoning, bookkeeping, numbers, sitting at a desk, or running off copies of the church bulletin. But after studying this a bit more, it quickly became apparent I had no idea what the gift of administration really was. (I'll explain it soon.)

As I studied and learned more detail about each gift, it became easier to understand and accept those I have been given. It's important for us to look at them carefully, and let the Holy Spirit reveal truth to us.

• Mercy

The gift of **mercy** is about showing grace, forgiveness and compassion. The eyes of mercy are always roaming to and fro to see who may be suffering and in need of a touch from God, a kind word, an encouragement, or prayer—offered joyfully and not dutifully. The gift of mercy will be directed to someone in distress, often someone who has slipped through the cracks and is suffering alone. The act of mercy is done privately, humbly, never seeking acclamation or reward.

• Administration

The gift of administration is one of guidance or wise counsel to the Christian community, revealing and enabling others to see the leadership's vision. This person puts her own interests aside to bring the leadership's into focus. This gift is fundamental in aiding others to make the spiritual journey or mission being taught. There is a discernment required here, that all things the church leaders have set in motion are in accordance with God's Word.

Administration supports leadership, with skills in organization, clarification, inspiration, and compassion. This is key in setting others up to succeed in their own gifting.

• Giving

Who would ever think giving is a spiritual gift? But it is. Romans 12:8 says, *"If your gift is giving, then give generously."*

In 2007, my husband and I were called to begin a charitable work. During a visit to Haiti, we were overwhelmed by the tremendous need. It was beyond anything we could have imagined, and the realization shook us at how apathetic we had been toward our own blessings. It was time to give back. We really didn't have a clue what we were doing but knew beyond a shadow of a doubt God had called us to do something. We decided to go in obedience and, through God's power and provision, get a mission up and running.

We knew success must not depend on us, so we asked God to send Haitians of His choosing who could step into leadership roles as this project went forward. We also knew the costs of running a full-blown mission were going to grow into much more than we could manage ourselves. We are just simple folk, not skilled in marketing or fundraising or seeking platforms to reach the big givers, so we brought that to God. We told God we would joyfully do what He was calling us to, if He would provide the needed money. We were moving forward in faith in a powerful God to provide for His work in every way.

Well, it's now fourteen years later. The mission is completely run by a team of godly Christian nationals under the leadership of an amazing Haitian man, Wouillio Zamor. God brought us through the baby stages, bandaged our bleeding wounds from mistakes and learning, provided a wonderful Haitian staff, and every year touched the hearts and wallets of beautiful people who connected to what God was doing in a little village in Haiti. They gave generously, joyfully, and expectantly. Faithfully. Those people God called, and is still calling, have the gift of giving. They heard God's voice, saw the need, felt the tug on their heartstrings and gave. Hope Grows Haiti thrives today because of their gifting and their obedience!

You may be saying, whew! I'm glad I wasn't given that gift. Well, I actually believe this is one of those requirements given to all God's people at the point of redemption (Malachi 3:10). Scripture is clear we are *all* commanded to give back a portion of what we have, whether to our church, a mission, an organization, or privately to people in need. We do need to give back to God.

But the "gift" of giving comes with a passion for it. Tithing is just the beginning. These people are always looking for a place to honor God with their resources. It is a joy and a blessing. They give, as we all should, cheerfully (2

Corinthians 9:7). It may not always be a gift of money; it could be food, possessions, physical help with a project, or even babysitting. Sometimes we are called to give not out of excess, but out of a place of hardship and need. (And anyone can feel God speaking about this at any time and outside of this gifting.) But it is always given with pure motive and without thought of reward. Scripture promises great blessing to those faithful in this area.

• Helps

The gift of helps is often referred to as having a servant's heart. Here is Robert Clinton's definition from his book, *Spiritual Gifts.* "The gift of helps refers to the capacity to unselfishly meet the needs of others through very practical service."[14]

This gift is where the rubber meets the road. It is seen in every kindness, every self-sacrificing service, every meal for a sick neighbor, every loan of a vehicle, every snow-shoveled driveway, every drive to a chemo treatment, every hot coffee given to a homeless person, every bouquet of flowers given to someone sad, every roadside assistance offered, every pick up and drive home from church or groceries or doctor's appointments. It is washing the stack of dishes after a church function, sweeping the floors, or washing out the communion items. It's visiting the elderly who are stuck in long term care, giving time to listen to their life stories, and helping them feel valued, not forgotten. There are more ways to use the gift of helps than I have space to write them. This gift could be thought of as the least of giftings, but in heaven's eyes, it is the very heart of God.

---

[14] Robert Clinton,

Word gifts

According to Jon Thompson in his book *Convergence*, the word gifts clarify the nature, the action, and the purposes of God (he quotes from the work of Robert Clinton). Jon goes on to say that spiritual gifts are not about ego, duty, or identity but are always for the good of the community and to produce joy in us.[15] The categories of word gifts are teaching, encouragement, apostleship, leadership, shepherding, and evangelism.

• Teaching

The gift of teaching refers to exposing God's truth though the instruction of Scripture. When I was in teacher's college, the first thing rammed into us was the definition of teaching. It is "to instill in others an excitement and passion for learning, to provide the opportunity to experience it, and to equip them to continue this life-long journey on their own."

Teaching as a spiritual gift embraces all of these principles. A good teacher explains in an understandable way and makes sure there is a personal application evident in the process.

I'm sure we've all had a teacher in our past who could not break down a concept to the point of our understanding. Perhaps it was a math equation or Shakespeare or an economic principle, but no matter how hard we listened, we couldn't grasp understanding. It eluded us.

The God-given gift of teaching reaches beyond this, and through the working of the Holy Spirit, a person with the

---

[15] Jonathan Thompson, *Convergence.* C4 Church, 2018.

gift of teaching opens up what may seem the most confusing piece of Scripture so that we not only grasp the truth but are able to apply it in a life-changing way. A telltale result is the excitement created and a desire to learn more! I believe when this gift is used, the Holy Spirit steps in to the situation and His power works in the listeners, enabling them to understand. In other words, miracles happen. God's children are being prepared, trained, and equipped for wherever He wants them, through the obedience of Christians using their spiritual gifts.

If you are like me, you have experienced both types of teaching, recognizing the difference between the job of teaching and the gift of teaching, and perhaps share with me the joy of sitting under the latter.

But this specific gift comes with a warning. James3:1 says, *"Not many of you should become teachers, my fellow believers, because you know that we who teach will be judged more strictly."*

Be warned. Teachers will be held to a greater accountability. We need to pray for our spiritual leaders!

• Encouragement

Most of us have had an encourager in our lives at some time or another. Perhaps it is a teacher, a mom or dad, a close friend, or someone who keeps showing up with a hug or a casserole right when we need it. They seem intuitive to our issues and needs. Just when we are about to collapse, that card telling us how much we are loved and appreciated comes in the mail, and we are encouraged to persevere through our struggle.

Encouragement is the gift of taking time to listen. Encouragement is the gift of being able to hear between the words spoken to understand the words held back. It is not only sensing the problem at hand, but knowing how best to effortlessly bring God into the situation in a healing and restorative way.

Who knows how many, through receiving the gift of encouragement from a friend during a difficult time, went on to do great things for the kingdom of God!

• Apostleship
Some Bible scholars teach that apostleship can be used two ways: either as a position or office—such as an elder or deacon in the church—or as the gift, which is one of a messenger or courier.

Many see the gift of apostleship as missionary work or church planting or nurturing a fledgling project in response to God's call. This could be in social justice, among the poor and homeless, with foreign missions, or in a neighborhood Bible study.

Apostleship can be a commission on someone not even attached to a specific church or organization. Apostles are often just ordinary people God calls to extraordinary work. It usually just seems to happen, to simply come into being, and never from self-promoting or marketing.

This gift comes with humility, strength of character, a heart for God's people, an empowering relationship with Jesus, and always, with the desire that it be used for God's glory.

• Leadership

Leadership is vision. It is seeing what God wants to do and assembling the people with the right gifting to make it happen. It's motivating followers to accomplish the purposes of God.

Glancing through Scripture, we see in Exodus 3, Moses had the God-given gift of leadership, and so did many others, like David (2 Samuel 2), Daniel (Daniel 1:8-17), and Paul (Romans 1:1). But ladies, God not only calls men, He also calls His female creation, as He did with Abigail, David's wife (1 Samuel 25:1-42), Esther, a queen (Esther 4), Miriam, a prophetess (Numbers 12), Hulda, a prophetess (2 Kings 22), Rahab, a prostitute (Joshua 2), Deborah, a judge (Judges 4-5), Phoebe, a deacon (Romans 16), and Priscilla, a teacher (Acts 18). Many amazing women through the centuries have been given the gift of leadership, and God *still* calls His women to lead.

They say if you want to know if you are a leader, turn around and see if anyone is following! When God gives women the gift of leadership and they obey, He provides the followers!

Christians often confuse leadership with pastoring. They are not the same, yet are not mutually exclusive either. There is a difference, however, and we should be clear on this. Leaders are visionaries, and pastors are shepherds. Let's look at that gift.

• Pastor/Shepherd

My friend Michelle had a sheep farm. It wasn't a huge flock of sheep but enough to keep her busy. She loved her sheep, but they were a lot of work and monetarily not worth the effort. But because she loved them, she labored on to take care of them and do everything required to keep them safe.

Michelle fed and watered them, kept them warm in the winter, and provided pasture in the summer. She carefully tended to their wounds. If one was missing, Michelle called all her neighbors and searched until it was found. She built an electric fence about them to keep the wolves out and marked any with chalk that needed to be watched. She was a shepherdess. These were *her* sheep, and my friend would do whatever was needed to protect them from enemies so they could grow healthy and strong.

Shepherding is much like pastoring. These very same things are required in every church flock. Within that community, there is every need: of comfort in sorrow, of encouragement through difficulties, of protection against the enemy, of being fed spiritually, of healing from sickness and mental illness, of calming from fears, of giving direction, and of bringing in the wayward.

This is a tremendously needed gift. You don't have to be ordained to use your pastor/shepherd gift. In most churches, there are small study groups, home prayer groups, women's Bible study groups, grief share groups, divorce care groups, foreign student groups, and the need for elder care, childcare, and hospital or invalid visitation. If this is a gift you feel you've been given, ask Jesus to show you where to start, then talk to your pastor.

• Evangelism

Whenever I heard this gift talked about, I knew it was a great gift to have. As children of God, we are all called to be ready with a word to explain the hope within us, and I do try to share my faith whenever the opportunity presents itself, but this gift is more than that. This gift is an empowering of the Holy Spirit, enabling us to recognize occasions to speak up and speak out. It compels the Christian to say the exact thing needed to help someone through a struggle—perhaps to say what is needed to draw them into an honest conversation, revealing the truth of their disappointment or anger against God and addressing it. The woman with the gift of evangelism daringly shares her faith in spite of personal insecurity and speaks life and truth to those put in her path. She seeks opportunities, and God presents them, often. This is a unique calling.

Ephesians 4:11,12 identifies it. *"So Christ himself gave the apostles, the prophets, the evangelists, the pastors and teachers, to equip His people for works of service, so that the body of Christ may be built up."*

The evangelist is consumed with a burden for the unsaved and driven passionately to prayer on their behalf, continually seeking to share the gospel. They may be called to speak publicly or witness privately, but are always burdened by the broken heart of God over His lost sheep.

The evangelist seeks openings to speak clearly and in the power of the Holy Spirit to present the gospel. It could begin with or include personal testimony but always brings forth the good news Jesus came to share. Other gifting may open the door to receptiveness, but evangelism makes God's truth clear and brings the listener to a point of decision.

Here is a brief summary of God's truth in evangelism.

1. Because of our sin, which we were born into, we are doomed to be eternally separated from God. Romans 3:23 *"For all have sinned and come short of the glory of God."* God is holy and cannot look upon sin. The only way to obtain freedom from punishment and hell is through a sinless sacrifice made on our behalf. Romans 6:23 *"For the wages*

of sin is death, but the gift of God is eternal life in Christ Jesus our Lord."

2. Jesus was fully God, but willingly came as a human to be that perfect sacrifice.

3. He chose to give His life on the cross for our sins, making a way for us to be forgiven, and become part of the family of God. John 3:16 KJV *"For God so loved the world He gave His only begotten Son, that whoever believes in Him should not perish, but have eternal life."*

4. Through Jesus' death, His burial, His resurrection, and His ascension into heaven, death, sin, and the devil were defeated. Jesus had become the only way to the Father and eternal life. His death made it possible for us to be forgiven, to be changed, and to become part of the family of God. John 14:6 *"Jesus answered, "I am the way the truth and the life. No one comes to the Father except through me."*

5. In *accepting* this gift, we are freed from the horrors of hell and promised heaven and eternal life with Jesus and the saints.

Although the evangelist has a responsibility to use this gift, we need to remember that no one person can bring another into the kingdom of God. Only by the work of the Holy Spirit—perhaps in using the words of the faithful, but always through God's wisdom and power and revelation—can one become a true child of God.

After this has happened, the rest of us with our own spiritual gifts step in and, through teaching, shepherding, loving, supporting, befriending, encouraging, and comforting, do our part in guiding the new believer to a strong and growing relationship with Jesus. Our gifts are meant to work together to build up the family of God.

Power gifts

1 Corinthians 12:7-10 NRSV *"There are different kinds of gifts, but the same Spirit distributes them...Now to each one the manifestation of the Spirit is given for the common good. To one there is given through the Spirit a message of wisdom, to another a message of knowledge by means of the Spirit, to another faith by the same Spirit, to another gifts of healing by that one Spirit, to another miraculous powers, to another prophecy, to another distinguishing between spirits, to another speaking in different kinds of tongues, and to still another the interpretation of tongues."*

These gifts are called "power gifts" for a reason. They are unique in that they immediately bring the incredible power and presence of God into a situation. They include the gifts of tongues, healing, intercessory prayer, wisdom and discernment, faith, and prophecy. Let's take a quick look.

• Tongues
This gift has been controversial since the early church. There is much Scripture referring to it, including counsel and warnings.

"Tongues" is basically praying in a language you do not understand nor normally speak. This gift has two parts—speaking in tongues, or interpreting what was said. Scripture is clear that if there is the presence of one publicly, there must be the presence of the other. A word spoken in tongues must also be translated to be legitimate. 1 Corinthians, 12:27 *"If anyone speaks in a tongue, two or at the most three, they should speak one at a time, and someone must interpret."*

Interpretation is not required if tongues are spoken while worshiping or praying in private.

Some teach that all believers must be able to speak in tongues if they are truly filled with the Spirit, and some teach that this gift is no longer relevant, as it was given to the early disciples and apostles so they could preach to gathering crowds in their own languages.

The controversy has continued over the years and unfortunately has been an underlying cause of church splits, friendship fallouts, personal frustration, and even discouraged Christians leaving the faith.

I believe we need to see this as *one* of the *gifts* of the Spirit. A *gift* by nature is freely given. God in His wisdom gives and takes away as He sees fit. If He chooses to give someone this gift, that person should use it to God's glory, and if God gives you different gifts, don't feel less because He did not give you this one.

Regardless of how you have been taught or what you believe, do not, and I repeat, *do not* allow Satan to use this as a tool to make you question your faith or God's goodness and favor. If you allow Satan any freedom, he will take you to dark places of doubt, discouragement, and defeat. Leave this in Almighty God's hands.

• Healing
This healing could be physical, emotional, or mental. The gift is given when God chooses to restore someone from sickness to wholeness. In Scripture, Jesus continually

healed people of their illnesses, injuries, and diseases. I don't remember seeing anywhere that Jesus said no to anyone who approached Him for healing for herself or another. Jesus loved to bring wholeness to suffering people.

Jesus wants to heal today too. My husband and I pray over each other through colds, flu, and arthritis flare-ups, injured backs, failing eyesight, and debilitating headaches. We often see immediate, miraculous healing. But sometimes we don't. We ask in faith, then leave results in God's hands.

I never felt I had the gift of healing. Yet while working at our clinic in Haiti, when we have no medication or supplies to help sickness and deadly injuries that come in, I pray. A translator often prays with me. We ask God for miraculous healing for the patient because we have no other option. And we see miracles! There is no other explanation than that God intervened and healed in response to our plea.

We have seen the elderly covered in infected sores come back the next day with skin as smooth as a baby's bottom. We've seen life-threatening burns on a baby completely healed in days, a partially severed foot regenerated to where there was no sign of injury, gunshot wounds, machete trauma, and high blood pressure to the point of stroke—all healed through prayer!

God is still in the healing business, and we who can't claim this gifting can be given a miracle at a desperate time in response to a desperate prayer. So if you find yourself in that kind of situation, go right to God and ask!

James, the brother of Jesus, asked in James 5:14,15, *"Is anyone among you sick? Let them call the elders of the church to pray over them and anoint them with oil in the name of the*

Lord. And the prayer offered in faith will make the sick person well; the Lord will raise them up. If they have sinned they will be forgiven."

Elders may not necessarily have the gift of healing, but as official servants in this leadership position, God can give them this authority.

If you feel this is one of your gifts, then prepare yourself before the Lord in a time of cleansing, repenting, renouncing, and restoring. Ask God to lead you into this power gift as you humbly bow before Him. Always walk in this call with humility, asking each time for permission, then go forward in faith as He leads you.

• Intercessory prayer

As we have seen in a previous chapter, this is not regular prayer; it is powerful, intensified, and often comes upon one swiftly and without question. I have experienced this gift several times in my life (as shared in chapter 11). In each case, it has been given at a specific time for a specific purpose. Intercessory prayer is always given for another, usually for someone with tremendous, immediate need. The times I felt pressed to this prayer have been quite different in experience.

The first time I experienced it I was walking into a Tim Horton's for a much-needed coffee. As I moved toward the line, a young man looked my way and smiled. His smile did not reach his eyes, and I was drawn to deep sorrow reflected there. I smiled back and immediately felt the presence of the Holy Spirit calling me to pray for him. There was urgency with that call, a pressing into my heart, yet I did not know how to pray in detail. I slipped into line behind him, and began to silently plead the blood of Jesus over him and loose the will of heaven. As I asked for God's grace and mercy in his situation, I was suddenly engulfed in deep sadness—the sorrow, I believe, of God the Father for this young man. As I prayed, tears slid down my face. The harder I prayed, the faster the tears flowed. God wanted to heal him, He wanted to free him from something, and I had been called to bring him before the throne of grace for that miracle.

This has happened more than once, and the faces of those I have been called to pray over have not left me. I remember them every now and again and pray that God will keep His hand on them and do powerful things in their lives. Each time I do, I still tear up. God calls whomever He chooses to stand in the gap for another, at whatever time He chooses. Although we may not fully understand why, our only response is to obey.

• Faith

This may sound confusing to some, as we are all called to faith in Jesus, and Scripture makes it clear that *"without faith it is impossible to please God, because anyone who comes to Him must believe that He exists and that He rewards those who earnestly seek Him"* (Hebrews 11:6). But the *gift* of faith is something different, something more powerful.

This gift is like faith on steroids. I'm sure you've met people with this gift, and their unshakeable faith always stands out. They have the ability through their faith to encourage the rest of us to move forward, to take a stand, to trust God for something we're not sure of, to snuff out skeptics, and to know without a shadow of a doubt the will and purpose of God.

A good example of this faith is when David plucked five stones, picked up his slingshot, and ran toward the giant Goliath. He knew in his heart God wanted this enemy stopped and would empower anyone who stepped up to act. David moved in obedience on a faith that none other in that experienced army exemplified. That is a gifting of faith! And everyone benefited that day because of the faith and assurance of the young shepherd boy.

The gift of faith is often evident in children. They aren't all messed up with the "what ifs" and the "probably can'ts" and the "won't happens" of life. They simply believe. That is why Jesus said the kingdom of God is made up of followers like these little ones. They have the gift of faith! Sadly, life comes along, people disappoint, the enemy strikes again and again, and as children grow older, faith shrinks as doubt squeezes in. We've all witnessed it, if not experienced it ourselves.

The gifting of faith is something special. It is extraordinary, unexplainable, and unwavering in the face of obstacles. Yet with it there must be compassion, patience, and understanding for Christians struggling in theirs.

Jesus told His disciples in Matthew 17:20, *"Truly I tell you, if you have faith as small as a mustard see you can say to this mountain, 'Move from here to there,' and it will move. Nothing will be impossible for you."*

If you have seen a mustard seed, you'll know it is the smallest, most insignificant seed possible—a speck in the palm of your hand. Why would Jesus use this minuscule seed as a reference to faith when He taught how necessary faith was to please God?

Well, let me tell you a few things about that itty-bitty seed. First of all, it's a perennial. That seed will continually produce, year after year. When the roots are allowed to grow deep into the earth, that plant will continue to grow bigger and stronger than the year before. Second, the root system that grows from that little seed is incredible. Every year it spreads extensively into the soil, grabbing onto layers of rock, so the plant can withstand the greatest storms. Third, because of that tremendous root system, the plant becomes impossible to remove. You just can't pull it out! And fourth, that tiny mustard seed quickly grows into a solid tree bearing healthy, hearty produce that is used in varied ways. That minute seed, when allowed, becomes significant and impressive, allowing God's fulfillment of purpose through its design.

We need to stop measuring our faith by the size of the problem and keep our eyes on Jesus, the author of our faith, then no matter what the enemy puts in our way, we will stand strong.

• Wisdom and Discernment

The gift of spiritual wisdom can be explained as "knowing what is needed in a situation or for a specific person" and whether it calls for encouragement, advice, training, confession, or discipline. The people with this gift just know. It's a God-given understanding of spiritual things. It is prompted by the Holy Spirit as a special word, a powerful thought, or insightful information that brings understanding and healing into a situation.

With this gift, as with all other gifts, it is important to ask God for permission before speaking your thoughts and revelations into another person.

The gift of spiritual discernment often relates to the identification and recognition of either the Holy Spirit or evil spirits in any given situation. It gives insight into confusing activity. It can be used to discern motives behind actions, the source behind thoughts or words, the presence of angels or demons, and whether something is true or false.

We are told Satan often comes as an angel of light. He comes to deceive and confuse and is often extremely successful even with Christians. The gift of discernment is truly one of God's grace. When recognized as such and used within the power and permission of God, discernment can turn a potential triumph of Satan into a victory for the kingdom of God.

Others with the gift of discernment are sometimes able to see what is called the "invisible world." Dark angels and demonic beings appear to them in a recognizable form. Others can sense the presence of evil in a situation, recognizing it as demonically influenced, or when dealing with a person, instantly know they are demonized.

I have friends who have this gift, and it is not an easy gifting. Because Satan is a prowling lion, evil is all about us. The demonic world is exceedingly active. Christians with the gift of discernment are constantly aware of Satan's presence, often observing his dark angels at work. Most people cannot see or sense it, but those who can, find it a challenge. There are not a lot of people with whom to share these experiences. Not many want to hear those details. It can be a lonely and heavy gift to be given.

A very important point to remember about the gift of discernment and seeing is that this one and all other spiritual gifts are only given after people come to a personal knowledge of God. Only after a conversion or redemption experience will spiritual gifting take place. If you or someone you know claims to have had this gift from early childhood or birth, you can be sure it is not of God. It is from Satan, the great counterfeiter, and needs to be dealt with.

Fasting

Although this next topic is not listed with the gifts of the Holy Spirit, I want to look again at this act of obedience that may help to find your gifting or nurture one you already have into a growing, active, work of God—the discipline of **fasting**.

I had a sweet friend come to visit me one day and ask me if I had ever fasted. I scrunched up my face and said something like, "No! I'm pretty sure God won't ask me to fast because as soon as I hear the word, I'm instantly famished and start shoving food in my mouth. So I would be horrible at it." We both laughed and discussed it no more.

But not long after that, God put on my heart the desire to learn more about it, so I bought a book by Jentezen Franklin, simply called *Fasting*.[16] The day it arrived, I opened it to the first page and started reading. I could not put it down. Oh, the things I learned from this amazing book. What God taught me in those few days I will never forget. After finishing the book, I instantly felt called to do the exact thing I said I could never do. I started a fast, and I began to see God work in situations I had begun to believe were hopeless.

---

[16] Jentezen Franklin, *Fasting.* Charisma House, 2010.

God introduced the idea of fasting as far back as the Garden of Eden, when Adam and Eve were allowed to eat of all the fruit trees but one. That one they were not to eat. Isn't it funny how Satan used that small restriction to make Eve resentful and cause them to sin? He was able to convince her without much trouble that God was holding out on them. They should be able to eat whatever they wanted, whenever they chose. He made God look mean, and they felt hard done by. Adam and Eve put their stomach before their relationship with God and ended up eating themselves out of God's blessing, provision, protection, and presence. (Note that Satan is defeated and only has the power God allows, but he's been given permission to piggy-back on our disobedience and defiance to do serious damage. We see that in this instance, we see it over and over through the pages of Scripture, and we see it in our own lives!)

Fasting is an obedience that God honors. It is a sacrifice and an act of worship that takes our mind from the all-consuming needs of our stomach and brings a greater sensitivity to hearing from God in new and exciting ways. Fasting releases the anointing and the favor and blessing of God in ways we may not have seen before.

Jesus fasted. He fasted for forty days before His temptation by Satan, knowing there is a supernatural power that can only be bound or released through this discipline. Moses fasted for forty days and received the Ten Commandments during this time. Esther called for a three-day fast of all Jews to prepare King Xerxes' heart to save them from annihilation, and they were saved. Hannah fasted while asking God to give her a child, and it was given. The prophet Joel called his people to fast three different times in regard to seeking God's redemption from their sins. Anna, Judah, Ezra, Nehemiah, Jehoshaphat, David, Daniel, Paul, Peter, and the city of Nineveh are also among those whose fasts are recorded in Scripture, ending in a mighty work of God in each situation.

In case your face is scrunched up in disgust at the thought, let me give you more details from Jentezen Franklin's book. Fasting is always about the abstinence of food, but it doesn't always have to be *all* food. Many of my fasts have been abstaining from select food, like sweets or bread or dairy; Daniel's fast was from red meat, wine, and delicacies. We can fast from one meal, one day, or one week...whatever we feel called to. It is in the impact of this sacrifice we are reminded to turn our heart to God's. Each time the craving or hunger pangs show up, we take it as a prompting to pray. Each time we are called to fast, there is a purpose in it: a specific need for which we must dedicate much prayer. Sometimes it is simply a desire to hash out a pressing issue with God and find peace.

But remember, fasting is not a way of manipulating God, it is a way of seeking God, petitioning Him, praising Him, and preparing to hear His heart. The Bible tells us He rewards all who diligently seek Him because He finds our steps of faith pleasing. When we put Him first, He will put the rest in order.

A quick warning needs sharing here. Before launching yourself on a fast, please make sure this is something you are physically able to do. If you have health issues you may want to talk to your doctor first and get his blessing.

Questions

Do you see yourself in any of the gifts mentioned above?

Describe how you have used that gifting and how you've seen God's blessing through it. If you were not able to identify your gifts, pray about it, seeking direction from God. Ask a friend what they see in you regarding these areas. Think about the times you feel God's presence and power in your life while building up others in the kingdom.

While reading through the details on each gifting, did you see someone else reflected in any of these areas? Why not make a note to share with them what has been revealed to you about their gifts? It may be just the encouragement they need.

How do you feel now about fasting? Is your heart open to that call? Write a prayer asking God to give you the strength to enter into this act of worship, sacrifice, and obedience. Ask your heavenly Father to reveal the purpose He has created you for and the gift He is giving you to accomplish it!

Chapter Thirteen
Eyes to See

This chapter may deviate a bit from what we have been learning, but I've found this exercise an exciting one and want to share it with you.

As we find ourselves on a more meaningful journey—armed and ready to deal with the enemy—reading Scripture becomes a different pilgrimage. Our new spiritual eyes begin to see the devil's hand in many places and occasions we would never have expected, and God's powerful intervention on behalf of His children. Even Bible stories heard since childhood have a greater impact when we identify the presence of good and evil behind the event.

Not long ago my husband, Gord, had eye surgery. He'd suffered for decades with deteriorating vision, and finally a surgeon felt he could help. The day came when Gord went to the clinic, and his right eye went under the knife. His cataracts were removed and his eye's lens was cut out and replaced with a new one. When he was able to remove the bandages, words failed him as he looked at the vividness of the sky and trees, read all the signs by the road, and appreciated the colors of food on his plate. He had not even realized the dullness of the world he had been living in until the new lens was inserted. The next week, his other eye was given the same treatment, and his world became a place of even greater awe and wonder. Everything Gord now experienced revealed God's majesty, His power, and His beauty in unexpected places. That's exactly what our new spiritual lenses do for us!

To illustrate that, I'd like to take a look at a familiar Bible story using the new spiritual lenses we're beginning to enjoy. It's the story of David and Goliath, found in 1 Samuel 17.

This is not just a battle between two nations and two people anymore; it's now a battle between good and evil, heaven and hell. As we cheer from the sidelines, our new spiritual lenses give us a glimpse into the invisible world that permeates all things. We see spiritual warfare in a new way.

After you read through the story, we'll go back and skim through the timeline of events and make it personal. We'll regard Goliath as Satan and David as us.

Go ahead. We'll wait for you to read 1 Samuel 17.

Now, let's look at it more closely, and see the deeper message. We'll review events, and then draw an application.

The Story of David and Goliath

1. The Philistine army, Israel's fiercest enemy, has assembled on a hill across a valley from the Israelite camp in an attempt to intimidate God's army and force their hand to battle. Each day, Goliath steps out from the crowd. He is nine feet tall! His armor covers his whole body and is made of impenetrable bronze.

There are many times in our lives when Satan makes his presence known and demands a showdown—a confrontation forcing us to take a stand. Let's be ready! Satan can look fierce, powerful, and undefeatable. But we know God is greater!

2. Goliath shouts, "I'm a Philistine, and you are only servants of Saul!" Goliath continues his rant, ending with, "I defy the ranks of Israel!"

The enemy is arrogant and haughty, (which got him thrown out of heaven), and does not want to acknowledge the living God. But, take on God's people, you take on God!

3. David shows up, drops off his cargo and runs to the battlefront to see his brothers and find out what is happening.

He is fearless in the face of battle. So are we!

4. David's brothers are not glad to see him, and ridicule him, making fun of his size and inexperience in war.

Not all of God's people are supportive or happy about our spiritual journey. Sometimes they may feel threatened and perhaps condescending about our experiences and growth. But that must not deter us. Keep on growing in God's Word!

5. Goliath steps forward with his usual scathing tirade.

Evil is aggressive, persistent, and often predictable. But God has given us authority over Satan.

6. The Israelites know the enemy is defying Israel, God's chosen people, but fear is a greater force with them than the power of God.

Defying Israel was defying God himself, but King Saul was weak and faithless, unable to spur his army on. There was a time when Saul would have taken on Goliath himself, but because he was no longer trusting in God, he was overwhelmed with fear, and so was his army. Our walk of faith influences many also. Let's walk strong.

7. David asks what the reward is for removing this disgrace from Israel. He learns the reward is the king's daughter.

The king was giving up his beautiful daughter, but that had not been enough to coax any soldier to step up to the fight. God offered up His Son to give salvation, eternal life, and victory to any who choose to accept the invitation, yet so few do. Have we?

8. David's brothers rebuke him, rage at him, and ridicule him. They call him a pathetic little shepherd boy.

Proverbs 18:21 (MSG) says, "Words have the power of life and death, they are either life-giving or murderous, they are either poison or fruit. You choose." The brothers' words revealed their hearts. Perhaps the ridicule from them stemmed from jealousy or resentment. Bitterness will always make us say hurtful things, exposing the condition of our heart. Our words will always betray us.

9. David leaves his brothers and goes to talk to someone who will respond more kindly.

Do we drive family away with unkind words or harsh judgments? Or are we the one the others always pick on? David kept going in his quest for understanding, not willing to be discouraged by his brothers. We should remember this example and not let anyone's harsh words or judgments keep us from seeking God's purpose and plan for us.

10. King Saul hears about David's inquiries and sends for him. David says, "Don't lose heart, my king. I will go and kill the giant!"

David stood out in the crowd. Perhaps God's pleasure and presence in him caused that? David also had no qualms about this challenge. He was confident and strong in his faith in the living, loving, protecting God. Are we? Not just sometimes, but even in the face of trials and challenges?

11. King Saul discourages David, saying he is just a boy, and Goliath has been fighting for many years, now a giant in both size and experience.

Saul looked only at the problem, not recognizing the solution God had provided. Where is our focus in the midst of challenges and trials?

12. David replies, "When I kept my father's sheep, bears and lions came to steal them. I would grab their hair and kill them. This non-Jew can't scare me! If God can save me from lion's and bear's paws, He can save me from Goliath's big mitts!"

David had a history with God's saving power. His faith was solid because of already seeing God step in to save him in the past. His faith was unshakeable. No doubts, no need to stop and ask God if it was okay to fight this giant, because David knew God's heart and had experienced His might. With God there is only black and white, good and evil, right and wrong. David knew what he had to do, and he knew God would save him.

13. David grabs his slingshot and chooses five smooth stones, then confidently moves toward the enormous enemy. The giant walks toward the boy. David shouts as he now runs toward Goliath, *"You come against me with sword and spear? Well I'm coming against you in the name of the LORD Almighty whom you have defied!"*

We also come against Satan in the name of the Lord Almighty, whom Satan continues to defile, and we can be just as sure of victory as David was so long ago. God is the same, yesterday, today, and forever.

14. David shouts again that the victory will be God's, not by man or man-made equipment.

God will use a willing servant who is passionate about God's heart and excited about what God wants to accomplish.

15. David draws out a stone for his slingshot and fires it, hitting Goliath smack-dab in the middle of his forehead. He falls face down in the dirt.

Yay! We all cheer. God gave the boy His Holy Spirit, accurate aim, confidence, and victory. God gives the same to us! As we go in His name to take our stand against Satan and the devastation he's causing in us and in our families, we too will see victory.

16. Dave (as my grandson calls him) stood over Goliath, took the giant's sword, killed him, then cut off his head. Then Israel, realizing the opportunity, ran to overtake the Philistines, chasing them for miles until the enemy camp had been vanquished!

When we take a stand in Jesus' name, victory over evil will follow. That victory can also have a rippling effect, just as it did for the tribe of Israelites. The sword we wield is the sword of the Spirit, Scripture. As we read, study and memorize the Word of God, we'll be able to wield it more decisively and accurately.

17. David brought Goliath's head to Jerusalem but kept Goliath's weapons.

We need to keep a journal of the victories and answers to prayer we see in our journey, recording battles fought and won in Jesus' name.

18. As King Saul watched these events take place, he asked his chief commander, Abner, "Who is that boy?" Abner shrugged his shoulders. Saul responded, "Find out!"

The world is watching us. When they see God's power in our life they too will ask questions. "What makes her so different? I need to know more about her faith." God uses our obedience to speak to others.

19. When David returned, Abner presented him to King Saul. The king asked one question. "Whose son are you?"

Scripture tells us (1 Peter 3:15) to be ready with a word to answer when we are asked about the hope that is within us—whose daughter we are—because when spiritual victory becomes a part of our everyday life, it will be noticed, and people will want to know more. God draws other women to spiritual victory when they see ours!

This story is just one of the many incredibly true experiences in the Bible. You could do this exercise with any one of them, like Daniel in the lions' den, Queen Esther, Elijah and the fire from heaven, Jacob and Esau, Balaam, Jonah, and Samson and Delilah. These stories will come to life, revealing God's incredible power over the enemy, time and time again.

Since Scripture was written, there have been myriads of *real life* stories told about men and women living victorious lives and seeing God's hand of miracles. God is not just the God of the Bible, He is God of all time. He's Alpha and Omega, the beginning and the end. He is Creator of heaven and earth and all that is within it. His Word stands forever, and His power fills the universe. He has given us, His godly women, the strength to stand firm against the enemy to see him defeated in our lives, and in those under our authority.

In Jeremiah 9:17, the prophet utters a powerful prayer. He is sorrowful over the wayward nation of Israel. They have left worshiping the living God and turned to worshiping idols, which means Satan and his dark angels. Jeremiah cries out to God,

"Call for the mourning women to come and raise a wailing over us that our eyes may run down with tears and our eyelids flow with water!"

Women of God, the prophet Jeremiah recognized our part in God's plan of healing and redemption. Tears come from sorrow, brokenness, inner anguish, or repentance. When the Holy Spirit calls this into our heart for loved ones, for friends, for our church, or for our nation—any who desperately need a touch from God—our tears bring about a releasing and an outpouring of God's power. There is a time for holy tears; it was then, and it is now. Precious women, we are being called once again. We have much to contribute, and we are equipped!

I personally believe Jeremiah had at some time witnessed the power of God through redeemed, engaged, committed women, and pleaded with God to do it again to bring their lost nation to a place of repentance and salvation. That plea remains before the Father and beckons us today.

God is calling us to step out and step up into our destiny of warrior women. Let's rise to the call and see the blessing of God's deliverance. We can do this! And may God have the honor, the glory, and the praise. Amen.

A Final Encouragement

Thank you for taking this journey with me. I pray it has drawn you into a closer and more powerful walk with our amazing God. I'm also praying for such victory in your life that you become brave, bold, fearless, and dangerous to the enemy!

I also want to encourage you to start a Bible study on your own or with a friend or two. There are many different topics and styles of studies on the Christian market, written by amazing Bible teachers that you'll enjoy. There is also an online study, www.becomedevoted.com, directed by my daughter, Becki Baxter, and a team of godly young women. If you prefer a simpler method, I suggest you choose one book in the Bible at a time, and as you read, ask yourself these three questions. First, what is this passage revealing about God? Second, what is this passage saying to me? And third, how does God want me to apply this information to bring change into my life, my relationships, and my walk with Him?

Keep a sturdy journal and pretty pen beside you as you go, recording your answers and whatever you feel the Holy Spirit is revealing. At the end of each book, chapter, or section that delivered a personal impact, write a prayer sharing your heart with the Father.

Warrior Woman is just a glimpse into the incredible depths of spiritual warfare. There are many other works written by devoted men and women of God. I'm going to share a few below that I have enjoyed. So if you have heard God speaking to you through these pages and have a desire to go deeper, learning more on this topic, I suggest finding one or *all* of these books to add to your personal library.

May you walk in peace, live in joy, run in faith, and shine brightly for Jesus!

Your friend,
Heather
www.heatherraerodin.com

Jeremiah 31:13 *"Then maidens will dance and be glad...I will turn their mourning into gladness: I will give them comfort and joy instead of sorrow."*

Suggested Reading

Anderson, Neil, *The Bondage Breaker.* Harvest House Publishers, 2000.

Barsness, Jean, Anywhere, Anytime, Any Cost. Word Alive Press, 2016.

Bubeck, Mark I., *The Adversary.* Moody Publishing, 2013.

Bubeck, Mark I., *Overcoming the Adversary.* Moody Publishers, 1984.

Hayford, Jack, *Penetrating the Darkness.* Chosen Books, 2011.

Ingram, Chip, *The Invisible War.* Baker Books, 2015.

Kraft, Charles H., *Defeating Dark Angels.* Chosen Books, 2016.

Kraft, Charles H., *I Give You Authority.* Chosen Books, 2012.

Lutzer, Erwin W., *God's Devil.* Moody Publishers, 2015.

Meyer, Joyce, *Battlefield of the Mind.* WarnerFaith, 2002.

Thompson, Jonathan, *Convergence.* C4 Church, 2018.

Wiersbe, Warren W., *The Strategy of Satan.* Tyndale House, 1979.

Appendix A

What's in a name?

My father gave me the name Heather, which held great meaning for him. He was born in Scotland and grew up with the heather growing on the moors. The name brought memories and images of a happy time in his life, and in a way it made me feel important.

Names are important to God and carry specific meaning. Different places in Scripture reveal angels foretelling a birth along with what the child's name will be. Two good examples are John the Baptist and Jesus!

We have talked about God knowing our names and calling us by them as He did with Mary, Martha, Samuel, Moses and Jacob. Let's look at God's names and learn a little more about Him. Take the time to look up the scriptures for each one, then research the name to find out the meaning.

Elohim: John 17:3

Jehovah: Genesis 2:4

El-Shaddai: Exodus 3:14,15

Jehovah Jireh: Genesis 22:14

Jehovah Rophe: Exodus 15:26, Jeremiah 30:17

Jehovah Nissi: Numbers 13

Jehovah M'Kaddesh: Deuteronomy 7:6, Leviticus 20:8

Jehovah Shalom: Judges 6:24

Jehovah Tsidkenu: 2 Corinthians 5:21, Ephesians 6:14

Jehovah Rohi: Isaiah 40:10,11, Psalm 23, John 10:11

Jehovah Shammah: Deuteronomy 31:6, Hebrews 13:5

Abba: Mark 14:16

These few names of God reveal His power, His majesty, and His glory, showing He is able to meet every need of those He created, those who call on Him. When we pray to the appropriate name of God for a specific need, it's personal and draws special attention to that quality. See if you can find more names of God.

Appendix B

What's in a name? (continued)

As God has many names, Satan has some too. Scripture reveals several to us. Here are a few and their meanings. Take time to look each reference up in one or two different versions. Circle the ones that show up most often in your life. Write out the verses that coincide with the names you have circled.

Lucifer: son of the morning or shining one, Isaiah 14:12

Satan: adversary, 1 Thessalonians 3:18

Devil: slanderer, 1 Peter 5:8

Evil one: 1 John 5:19

Beelzebub: lord of the flies, Matthew 12:24

Tempter: 1 Thessalonians 3:5

Prince of this world: John 12:31

Prince of the power of the air: Ephesians 2:2

Accuser of the brethren: Revelation 12:10

Father of lies: John 8:44

What are demons like?

They are individuals with jobs and purposes.

They have a will. Matthew 12:43-45 *"When an unclean spirit goes out of a man, he goes through dry places seeking rest, and finds none. Then he says, 'I will return to my house from which I came.'"*

They have the ability to speak and have understanding. Mark 1:24 *"Let us alone! What have we to do with You, Jesus of Nazareth?"*

They have names. Mark 5:9 *"'What is your name?' And he answered, saying, 'My name is Legion, for we are many.'"*

They believe in God. James 2:19 *"You believe that there is one God. You do well. Even the demons believe, and tremble."*

They have false doctrines. 1 Timothy 4:1 *"In latter times some will depart from the faith, giving heed to deceiving spirits and doctrines of demons."*

They have tremendous powers through those they occupy and oppress. Acts 19:16 *"Then the man in whom the evil spirit was, leaped on them, overpowered them, and prevailed against them, so that they fled out of that house naked and wounded."*

They have supernatural powers. Revelation 16:14 *"For they are the spirits of devils working miracles, which go forth unto the kings of the earth and of the whole world."*

In the Lord's prayer, Jesus tells us to pray for deliverance against forces of evil...*every day*! Satan and his kingdom are forces of evil.

More Books from Heather

PRINCE OF
VOODOO

BREAKING
THE CHAINS

HEATHER RODIN

ACTING
BADLY

A SORCEROR'S STORY OF
REDEMPTION

HEATHER RODIN

Available for purchase through:
www.appointeddevotional.com

Printed in the United States
by Baker & Taylor Publisher Services